S0-BBC-200

The Evolution of Central Banks

The Evolution of Central Banks

Charles Goodhart

The MIT Press
Cambridge, Massachusetts
London, England

The first edition of this book, under the title *The Evolution of Central Banks: A Natural Development?*, was issued in 1985 by the Suntory-Toyota International Center for Economics and Related Disciplines, The London School of Economics and Political Science, © 1985 Charles Goodhart.

This book was set in Palatino by Asco Trade Typesetting Ltd. in Hong Kong, and printed and bound by Halliday Lithograph in the United States of America.

Library of Congress Cataloging-in-Publication Data

Goodhart, C. A. E. (Charles Albert Eric)
  The evolution of central banks.

  Bibliography: p.
  Includes index.
  1. Banks and banking, Central—History. 2. Banks and banking, Central.
3. Free banking. I. Title.
HG1811.G62 1988   332.1'1'09   87-36632
ISBN 0-262-07111-8
ISBN 0-262-57073-4 (pbk.)

Contents

Preface

For seventeen years, 1968–1985, I worked as an economic adviser on domestic monetary affairs in the Bank of England. For much of that period the main issues on the agenda concerned such topics as the stability and predictability of the demand-for-money function and velocity, and associated questions of the relative merits of alternative monetary targets, rules versus discretion, and the choice between various kinds of monetary control mechanisms.

During the last few years of my stay in the Bank, however, it seemed to me that the focus of interest among academic monetary economists was shifting, away from concern about appropriate rules of conduct for Central Banks, toward even more fundamental issues about the rationale for having such an institution in the first place.

This latter question had last been widely discussed in the nineteenth century, e.g., at the time of the debate between the Banking and Currency Schools and subsequently by Bagehot in the United Kingdom, and had been largely dormant since then. Now, however, there has been a revived interest both in such earlier monetary theorizing and in the earlier historical episodes that might illuminate the question of how successful "free banking," i.e., in the absence of a Central Bank, might be.

As a monetary historian, I found such revived interest delightful; but as a monetary economist, and an erstwhile Central Bank economist, I found the arguments of those who claimed that Central Banks represented an unnecessary, interventionist, artificial, inflationary intrusion into an otherwise idyllic, efficient, self-equilibrating, natural system of "free banking" to be misconceived.

I set out, therefore, to try to correct the balance, by showing how the role and functions of Central Banks have evolved *naturally* over time, and play a necessary part within the banking system. In line with much of the recent literature on this subject, I devote a sizable proportion of this book to historical study of the development of Central Banking, but I attempt, in some of the later chapters, to bring the analysis up to date. In fact, there has recently been a proliferation of theoretical advances in our understanding of the nature of banking, and hence of Central Banking.

Like my subject, my own work has evolved over time, rather than conforming to an initially planned structure. It began in the form of a couple of associated private background papers, which I circulated to some colleagues in the Bank. Then, as I began to become more interested in the history and early literature, the essays lengthened, and became festooned with footnotes and appendices. By the time that I left the Bank, the work extended to monograph length, and was published, as such, by the Suntory-Toyota International Centre for Economics and Related Disciplines (ST/ICERD) at the London School of Economics in 1985.

While I felt reasonably content with the historical parts of this monograph, I was concerned that the more theoretical chapters, primarily chapters 3, 6, and 7, needed some further extension and elaboration. In particular, I subsequently wrote another paper on this subject, "Why Do Banks Need a Central Bank?" *Oxford Economic Papers* (March 1987), and I have taken the opportunity of the republication of this monograph by The MIT Press to add additional material from this paper to the present chapter 7 and to reorganize the monograph's structure and form, partly to cut down on its multiplicity of footnotes and appendices.

Acknowledgments

Much of this research work was done while I was at the Bank of England, but at all stages it has remained my own independent initiative. It has been neither commissioned, supported, nor endorsed by the Bank, and the study has only used material publicly available to any economist. The views expressed are solely my own personal responsibility, and should not be ascribed to the Bank of England, or to the International Centre for Economics and Related Disciplines (ICERD), or to the London School of Economics and Political Science. I did, however, show earlier versions to some colleagues within the Bank as well as to many outside, and I am grateful for comments and suggestions from John Flemming, Robin Matthews. Leslie Presnell, Lionel Price, Jack Revell, Richard Timberlake, and Lawrence White.

I worked on this monograph for a couple of years, enlarging, extending, and continuously rewriting it. I am most grateful to Sheila Gibbs for patiently, accurately, and rapidly undertaking the secretarial work that enabled the exercise to be completed. Finally I am grateful to Eric Sosnow for creating the conditions that allowed this work to come forward in this form.

The Evolution of Central Banks

Chapter 1
Introduction

Although Central Banks would appear to be firmly established in all major countries, academic economists have been far from convinced that these institutions are necessary, or even desirable in an optimal state of affairs. It is notable that two of the main authors on the role and functions of central banking in the United Kingdom, Walter Bagehot in *Lombard Street* and Vera Smith in *The Rationale of Central Banking*, both preferred free banking in theory[1] even though they both recognized that the abolition of the Bank of England in practice would appear an impractical and farfetched proposal. Yet, despite this, many of the recent group of economists who have been examining the option of free, or competitive, banking, and questioning the need for, and functions of, a Central Bank (in a critical spirit) have emphasized their view that this issue has been foreclosed and ignored by other economists.[2] Thus Klein (1974) begins his paper with the claim that "few areas of economic activity can claim as long and unanimous a record of agreement on the appropriateness of government intervention as the supply of money" (p. 423).

Discussions on free banking (i.e., banking freed from the presence of a Central Bank), and the role, if any, for a Central Bank, were particularly lively during the early and mid-nineteenth century; indeed, Vera Smith's excellent book largely consists of a historical restatement of the course of these controversies and discussions during the nineteenth century in the United Kingdom and Europe. Subsequently the subject fell dormant, and issues appeared largely settled. More recently, however, there has been a revival of discussion and interest on these issues. This has had several sources. Both Friedman and Hayek have queried whether the exercise of discretionary monetary policy by a Central Bank is desirable. If such discretionary policy was to be abandoned, however, and replaced by a policy rule, or by laissez-faire, what role, if any, would be left for a Central Bank? Although both Friedman and Hayek independently criticize the exercise of discretionary monetary policy, they have markedly different views on the preferred alternatives. Thus Hayek (1978) doubts whether a rule for monetary growth could be established within the context of the existing structure of the banking system (see p. 77 especially); instead, he argues for free competition in the provision of notes and deposits by competitive banks within a laissez-faire system, in which there would be no need for any Central Bank (see pp. 101–102 especially). Friedman, on the other hand, advocates the adoption of a rule to determine the rate of growth of high-powered money, but continues to see a necessary role for the Central Bank within the system, in order to maintain the sanctity of contract, the prevention of fraud, and the effective working of the monetary system, in a world in which information is costly and scarce [see (1959), especially pp. 6–7].[3]

There has subsequently been a more general revival of interest in examining, questioning, and analyzing the structural necessity for, and functions of, a Central Bank. This is one aspect of a general reconsideration of the need, if any, for outside (governmental) bodies to intervene and regulate market forces. This also accords well with current trends in economic analysis, particularly among the rational expectations school, which advocates greater attention to the effect that different institutional structures, or regimes, particularly policy regimes set up by governments, may have on behavioral patterns in the various parts of the economy, and the functioning of the economy more broadly.[4] Prime examples of such studies are Klein (1974), Kareken and Wallace (1978), and King (1983), (1984b).[5] This theoretical literature has also been buttressed by a growing number of historical studies, which, inter alia, seek to reevaluate earlier historical experiences of free banking, especially in the United States and the circumstances surrounding the introduction of Central Banks. Such studies include Rockoff (1975), Timberlake (1978), Vaubel (1984a), White (1984b), and Rolnick and

Weber (1983). Also see the bibliography provided by White in the appendix to chapter 3 and the supplement to that appendix in Salin (1984b), King (1983), and Timberlake (1984). The main conclusion of several of these exercises has been to suggest, upon such re-examination, that a free banking system, or at least a monetary system without a Central Bank, was not so bad after all.

In this approach, therefore, a comparison is drawn between a laissez-faire, free-banking regime and a regime in which a Central Bank is constituted, under one, or another, operating regime, such as the Gold Standard, a fixed monetary growth rule, or discretionary monetary policy. By implication, Central Banks have been introduced as a policy step, an intervention from outside, and could, by some such similar step, be changed, or even removed entirely in future. Anyhow, the appropriate role and functions, if any, of a Central Bank has now become an issue in the literature, alongside the appropriate design of monetary regimes.

This literature has followed other associated paths. One such has been to examine and to criticize the nature of the incentives and the rewards/penalties incorporated in the structure of Central Banks themselves. The motive for such work lies in a perceived contrast between the individual personnel of Central Banks, who are, at present, generally seen to be as able and desirous of the public good as their confreres outside, with (what are taken to be) the end results of their operations, e.g., endemic and accelerating inflation, volatile monetary and financial conditions, etc. The question is, therefore, raised whether, somehow, the risk/reward structure and/or the decision-making process is systematically badly organized. For an example on the poor organization of the decision-making process, see Mayer;[6] on the question of potentially inappropriate risk/reward structures, see the various papers by Acheson and Chant, Buchanan, Friedman (1982), Santoni, and Schughart and Tollinson listed in the bibliography. Thus Buchanan (1984, p. 21) suggests that "for example, if the compensations of all employees of the monetary authority should be indexed so as to insure personal penalty from any departures from monetary stability, perhaps nothing more need be required by way of rules." Once upon a time Central Banks were more used to fulsome encomiums than to such criticism, as evidenced by this splendid purple passage from Patron (1911, p. 37): "In spite of the complications of its task, we shall find the Bank always the leader in matters of credit as well as of money, unremittingly faithful to the great mission which the State intrusts to it, and its mastery of which we all acknowledge."

To return to the main theme, however, there are, perhaps, two main strands in the case for free banking, which case is described in greater detail in chapter 2. The first argument involves a frontal attack on discretionary monetary management. If such management is to be undertaken at all, it needs an institution to carry it out. This institution would be, in effect, a Central Bank. The argument between discretionary management and some kind of "rule" has, however, been discussed endlessly elsewhere, and it is not the purpose of this book to discuss that issue further.

Instead, this book seeks to follow a second strand of argument about the role of a Central Bank. This latter argument concerns the question of whether the introduction of an outside agency to regulate and control the banking system represents an undesirable intervention in the otherwise satisfactory working of a free-market system in the banking industry. The main purpose of this book is to consider this latter issue, examining both the analytical arguments and the historical evidence.

When the first Central Banks were founded in Europe, there was, however, little, or no, consideration, or attention, given to the possibility of these banks playing a supervisory role in relation to other banks. Instead, the initial impetus was much more basic, generally relating to the financial advantages that governments felt that they could obtain from the support of such a bank, whether a state bank, as in the case of the Prussian State Bank, or a private bank, e.g., the Bank of England. This function naturally involved favoritism, often supported by legislation, by the government for this particular bank in return for its financial assistance—see, for example, Cameron (1967).

An associated purpose for which these early Central Banks were founded was to unify what had become in some cases, e.g., in Germany, Switzerland, and Italy, a somewhat chaotic system of note issue, to centralize, manage, and protect the metallic reserve of the country, and to facilitate and improve the payments system. While these latter functions were seen as having beneficial economic consequences, the ability to share in the profits of seignorage and the greater centralized control over the metallic (gold) reserves had obvious political attractions as well. In any case, prior to 1900, most economic analysis of the role of Central Banks concentrated on the issue of whether the note issue should be centralized, and, if and when centralized, how controlled by the Central Bank.

Once such Central Banks had been established, however, their central position within the system, their "political" power as the government's bank, their command (usually) over the bulk of the nation's metallic reserve, and, most important, their ability to provide extra cash, notes, by rediscounting made them become the bankers' bank: commercial banks would not only hold a large proportion of their own (cash) reserves as balances with the Central Bank, but also rely on it to provide extra liquidity when in difficulties. In several early cases, e.g., the Bank of England, this latter role had not been initially intended; in most cases of Central Banks founded in the nineteenth century the full ramifications of their role as bankers' bank were only dimly perceived at the time of their founding; these functions developed naturally from the context of relationships within the system.

Initially, indeed, the role of Central Banks in maintaining the convertibility of their notes, into gold or silver, was no different, nor seen as any different, from that of any other bank. Their privileged legal position, as banker to the government and in note issue, then brought about consequently, and, naturally, a degree of centralization of reserves within the banking system in the Central Bank, so it became a bankers' bank. It was the responsibility that this position was found to entail, in the process of historical experience, that led Central Banks to develop their particular art of monetary management.

Such management has had two (interrelated) aspects, a macro function and responsibility relating to the direction of monetary conditions in the economy at large, and a micro function relating to the health and well-being of the (individual) members of the banking system. Until 1914 such management largely consisted of seeking to reconcile, as best as possible, the need to maintain the chosen metallic standard on the one hand with concern for the stability and well-being of the financial system, and beyond that of the economy more widely, on the other. Then, as the various pressures of the twentieth century disrupted first the Gold Standard, and thereafter the Bretton Woods system of pegged exchange rates, the macroeconomic objectives of monetary management altered and adjusted. Yet at all times concern for the health of the financial system has remained paramount.

These interrelationships between the macro and micro functions of Central Banks, with the latter seen as being of primary importance, were well described in the paper "Federal Reserve Position on Restructuring of Financial Regulation Responsibilities" presented to the Bush Commission in December 1983 as follows:

> A basic continuing responsibility of any central bank—and the principal reason for the founding of the Federal Reserve —is to assure stable and smoothly-functioning financial and payments systems. These are prerequisites for, and complementary to, the central bank's responsibility for conducting monetary policy as it is more narrowly conceived. Indeed, conceptions of the appropriate focus for "monetary policy" have changed historically, variously focusing on control of the money supply, "defending" a fixed price of gold, or more passively providing a flow of money and credit responsive to the needs of business. What has not changed, and is not likely to change, is the idea that a central bank must, to the extent possible, head off and deal with financial disturbances and crises.
>
> To these ends, the Congress has over the last 70 years authorized the Federal Reserve (a) to be a major participant in the nation's payments mechanism, (b) to lend at the discount window as the ultimate source of liquidity for the economy, and (c) to regulate and supervise key sectors of the financial markets, both domestic and international. These functions are in addition to, and largely predate, the more purely "monetary" functions of engaging in open market and foreign ex-

change operations and setting reserve requirements; historically, in fact, the "monetary" functions were largely grafted on
to the "supervisory" functions, not the reverse.

The above argument, that the monetary (macro) functions of
Central Banks were largely grafted onto the supervisory functions,
and not the reverse, is of considerable importance. It implies that
the central core and rationale for the existence and operation of a
Central Bank is *not* necessarily to be found in its macro-economic
role in (discretionary) monetary management. Of course, if one
believes that such discretionary monetary management is desirable,
"a good thing," then one presumably needs a Central Bank to
conduct it, and that alone would then be sufficient justification for
the existence of a Central Bank. There remains, however, a flourish-
ing debate whether this macro function is best undertaken through
the discretionary management of a Central Bank, or whether it
would be achieved more successfully through adherence to some
"rule." Instead, the main concern of this study is with the need for
the micro functions of a Central Bank.

With the Central Bank coming to represent the ultimate source of
liquidity and support to the individual commercial banks, this micro
function brought with it naturally a degree of "insurance." Such
insurance, in turn, involves some risk of moral hazard, i.e., that
commercial banks, believing that they will be supported by Central
Banks from the consequences of their own follies, adopt too risky
and careless strategies. That concern has led Central Banks to become involved—to varying extents—in the regulation and supervision of their banking systems. Revell (1975, p. 127) notes that

> solvency [of commercial banks] must not be set at too low a
> level if monetary policy is to work at all. . . .
>
> There is one corollary to our line of argument that is worth
> noting. Prudential regulation and monetary policy are func-
> tions that are usually carried out quite separately. Even when
> a central bank is responsible for both, the interactions between
> the two are rarely considered. This is not a sensible situation.
> It would seem highly desirable for both functions to be carried
> out by the same body (inevitably the central bank) and with a
> clear realization of the connexions between them.

As lender of last resort, a central bank *has* to be involved in supervisory matters. The choice then rests between centralizing the administration of such functions in the Central Bank, or of having a multiplicity of supervisory agencies. This latter question is addressed again in chapter 5.

The adoption of this regulatory and supervisory role was, at least for those Central Banks founded in the nineteenth century, largely a natural and evolutionary development, and not one that they were programmed to undertake from their foundation. Indeed in England the legislative framework—the 1844 Bank of England Act—was to prove something of a barrier, and antipathetic, to the development of the regulatory functions by the Bank.[7] This act divided the Bank into two departments—the Issue Department, whose note issuing function was to be closely constrained by strict rules (to maintain the Gold Standard), and the Banking Department, which was intended and proposed to behave as an ordinary commercial bank.

As will be argued subsequently in this book, the micro functions of a Central Bank, in providing a central (and therefore economical) source of reserves and liquidity to other banks and hence both a degree of insurance and regulation, cannot be undertaken effectively, basically because of conflicts of interest, by a commercial competitor. The advantages of having some institutions(s) providing such micro Central Banking functions are such that, even in those countries without Central Banks, there was, as will be shown, a natural tendency toward them being provided, after a fashion, from within the private sector, e.g., by clearinghouses in the United States—see Timberlake (1984)—or by large, central *commercial* banks providing quasi-Central Bank functions. Nevertheless, because of conflict of interest, these functions were not, and cannot be, adequately provided by competing institutions. This latter needs to be emphasized because some critics of Central Banks, e.g., Timberlake (1984) and Selgin and White (1987), have suggested that clearinghouses would be capable of taking over several of the micro-structural functions of Central Banks.

Some Central Banks, mainly those that began their existence under private ownership, e.g., the Bank of England and Banca d'Italia, but also some that were subject to political oversight, e.g., Banque de France and the Commonwealth Bank of Australia, retained for a considerable time a large role in ordinary commercial banking. As will be argued subsequently, it was the metamorphosis from their involvement in commercial banking, as a competitive, profit-maximizing bank among many, to a *noncompetitive non-profit-maximizing* role that marked the true emergence and development of proper Central Banking. Indeed, competition between the other commercial banks and the Bank of England and the Banque de France, respectively, complicated, overshadowed, and tarnished their adoption of a regulatory role. This metamorphosis occurred naturally, but with considerable difficulty, in England, the difficulty arising in part from the existence of property rights in the profits of the Bank, and in part from concern about the moral hazards of consciously adopting a regulatory role (as evidenced in the arguments between Bagehot and Hankey). Conflicts between commercial banks and the Banque de France had been even more marked (than in England) in the first half of the nineteenth century, but, perhaps because it was more subject to "political" direction at the top, it was able to transform itself more easily into a non-competitive, regulatory institution in the latter half of the nineteenth century (see the appendix).

Other Central Banks, most often those set up later in the twentieth century, such as the Federal Reserve System (1913) or the Swiss National Bank (1905), or set up from the start as a publicly directed institution, e.g., the Reichsbank (1875), were designed from the outset to be non-competitive (with other commercial banks) and non-profit-maximizing (see the appendix). Naturally they found less *structural* difficulty in smoothly adopting a central regulatory role.

It is, however, perhaps surprising that some of those Central Banks that were designed from the outset to be noncompetitive have been relatively *less* involved in the *micro functions* of regulation. Thus the Reichsbank and the Swiss National Bank were intended from the start to regulate overall monetary conditions, but generally left the supervision (auditing, licensing, etc.) of individual commercial banks to separate governmental bodies. It may be that in those countries where conflicts of interest are more generally regulated, and supervision provided, by official bodies set up by legislation, there was a greater tendency to allocate this micro function to a separate body, whereas in countries where (self-) regulation has been provided more informally, this latter function (of micro monetary management) was more naturally adopted, in so far as it was undertaken at all, by the Central Bank. Even so, there seems no clearcut explanation of the varying extent to which Central Banks undertake the micro supervisory functions.

Considering the close interrelationship that generally exists between the macro and the micro regulatory functions of monetary management, and the inherent disadvantages of having a multiplicity of agencies acting in the same field, it is difficult for someone (who has been used to UK institutions) to see what advantages can be obtained from separating these functions, and hiving off certain micro supervisory and insurance functions to other official institutions (separate and distinct from the Central Bank). This subject remains of some practical concern; indeed, the Bush Commission in the United States reconsidered the overlapping boundaries of the various supervisory institutions there. The issue has, heretofore, generated surprisingly little academic and analytical interest, and will only be touched on lightly again in chapter 5. The structural changes in process in many countries, notably in Canada, the United States, and the United Kingdom, are now, however, making the subject of the design, coverage, and powers of the bodies supervising (parts of) the financial system a topical and important issue. I hope to be able to return to this topic in subsequent studies.

Instead, the purpose of the rest of this book is to combine theoretical analysis with historical example to explore the reasons for the development of Central Banks and the rationale for their existence. The following chapter restates the arguments *for* a return to "free banking" without having a Central Bank. Although current analytical discussion on the role of a Central Bank largely revolves around the issues of information availability (and the possibility of insurance), nineteenth-century discussion centered largely around the question of whether the market discipline imposed by a well-functioning clearinghouse would suffice to keep the banking system in order; this is discussed in chapter 3. For various reasons this discipline was not capable of preventing banking cycles and financial crises. In the meantime there were natural forces leading to the centralization of reserves with major banks at the center of the system, particularly, of course, those that had been endowed by legislation or government favoritism with special advantages. The development of such centralization, often through the correspondent system, on the one hand, and the provision of prudential insurance services by the major bank(s) at the center, on the other, was, however, severely restricted by conflicts of interest, so long as the major bank(s) at the center remained competitive, commercial banks. It was the large step to a noncompetitive, non-profit-maximizing role that was crucial for the emergence of true Central Banks; this is described in chapter 4.

Chapter 2
The Case for Free Banking

1. The Views of Bagehot and Henry Thornton

There are several strands in the case for free banking. The first is by analogy with the general case for free trade. If free trade and free competition are beneficial in other economic activities, what is so special about banking that justifies imposing special external controls, regulation, or supervision upon banks?[1] The onus for demonstrating a case for the benefits of Central Bank (or other external agency) regulation, supervision, etc., needs to be made by the putative supervisor. Currently, there is a groundswell of academic and political enthusiasm for the achievement of greater efficiency through the establishment of more competitive markets, and this again leads to a generalized preference for deregulation in financial, as well as other, markets, unless specific and compelling reasons for the continuation of any interference with laissez-faire can be adduced.[2] This argument was given much weight by Bagehot in *Lombard Street*, and played a considerable role in the French discussion on free banking in the 1860s (viz., the account of this debate in Smith, *The Rationale of Central Banking*, p. 88). Although the main theme of *Lombard Street* concerns the question of how the Bank of England might be educated and persuaded to perform its role better, Bagehot nonetheless felt that the banking system would perform better without having any Central Bank at all. He looked, instead, nostalgically toward a hypothetical banking system, a natural system in his view, of entirely independent banks (*Lombard Street*, p. 104):

> A large number of banks, each feeling that its credit was at stake in keeping a good reserve, probably would keep one; if

any one did not, it would be criticised constantly, and would soon lose its standing, and in the end disappear. And such banks would meet an incipient panic freely and generously; they would advance out of their reserve boldly and largely, for each individual bank would fear suspicion, and know that at such periods it must 'show strength', if at such times it wishes to be thought to have strength. Such a system reduces to a minimum the risk that is caused by the deposit. If the national money can safely be deposited in banks in any way, this is the way to make it safe.

Again (*Lombard Street*, p. 101):

Where there were many banks keeping their own reserve, and each most anxious to keep a sufficient reserve, because its own life and credit depended on it, the risk of the Government in keeping a banker would be reduced to a minimum. It would have the choice of many banks and would not be restricted to any one.

Again, (*Lombard Street*, pp. 275–277):

In a natural state of banking, that in which all the principal banks kept their own reserve, this demand of the bill-brokers and other dependent dealers would be one of the principal calls on that reserve. At every period of incipient panic the holders of it would perceive that it was of great importance to themselves to support these dependent dealers. If the panic destroyed those dealers it would grow by what it fed upon (as is its nature), and might probably destroy also the bankers, the holders of the reserve. The public terror at such times is indiscriminate. When one house of good credit has perished, other houses of equal credit though of different nature are in danger of perishing. The many holders of the banking reserve would under the natural system of banking be obliged to advance out of that reserve to uphold bill brokers and similar dealers. It would be essential to their own preservation not to let such dealers fail, and the protection of such dealers would therefore be reckoned among the necessary purposes for which they retained that reserve.

Nor probably would the demands on the bill brokers in such a system of banking be exceedingly formidable. Considerable sums would no doubt be drawn from them, but there would be no special reasons why money should be demanded from them more than from any other money dealers. They would share the panic with the bankers who kept the reserve, but they would not feel it more than the bankers. In each crisis the set of the storm would not be determined by the cause which had excited it, but there would be anything in the nature of bill broking to attract the advance of the alarm peculiarly to them. They would not be more likely to suffer than other persons; the only difference would be that when they did suffer, having no adequate reserve of their own, they would be obliged to ask the aid of others.

But under a one-reserve system of banking, the position of the bill brokers is much more singular and much more precarious.

Why, then, had the Bank of England become established as the Central Bank? According to Bagehot, this was *not* because it served any really useful *commercial* purpose, but because it had been imposed on the system by legislation, legislation that was in turn a reward for its role, notably in 1694, but also thereafter, in providing government finance at times of need on especially favorable terms. Thus:

> With so many advantages over all competitors, it is quite natural that the Bank of England should have far outstripped them all. Inevitably it became *the* bank in London; all the other bankers grouped themselves round it, and lodged their reserve with it. Thus our *one*-reserve system of banking was not deliberately founded upon definite reasons; it was the gradual consequence of many singular events, and of an accumulation of legal privileges on a single bank which has now been altered, and which no one would now defend.

This Hayekian facet of Bagehot has been largely forgotten, at least until recently. But, if Bagehot supposed the natural system so superior, why did he aim to improve the existing system, rather than change it entirely? Bagehot's answer to that is that that would not be practical politics (*Lombard Street*, pp. 66–67):

> But it will be said—What would be better? What other system could there be? We are so accustomed to a system of banking, dependent for its cardinal function on a single bank, that we can hardly conceive of any other. But the natural system— that which would have sprung up if Government had let banking alone—is that of many banks of equal or not altogether unequal size. In all other trades competition brings the traders to a rough approximate equality. In cotton spinning, no single firm far and permanently oustrips the others. There is no tendency to monarchy in the cotton world; nor, where banking has been left free, is there any tendency to a monarchy in banking either. In Manchester, in Liverpool, and all through England, we have a great number of banks, each with a business more or less good, but we have no single bank with any sort of predominance; nor is there any such bank in Scotland. In the new world of Joint Stock Banks outside the Bank of England, we see much the same phenomenon. One or more get for a time a better business than the others, but no single bank permanently obtains an unquestioned predominance. None of them gets so much before the others that the others voluntarily place their reserves in its keeping. A republic with many competitors of a size or sizes suitable to the business, is the constitution of every trade if left to itself, and of banking as much as any other. A monarchy in any trade is a sign of some anomalous advantage, and of some intervention from without.
>
> I shall be at once asked—Do you propose a revolution? Do you propose to abandon the one-reserve system, and create anew a many-reserve system? My plain answer is that I do not propose it. I know it would be childish. Credit in business is like loyalty in Government. You must take what you can find of it, and work with it if possible.

Again (*Lombard Street*, pp. 105—106):

> Nor would any English statesman propose to 'wind up' the Bank of England. A theorist might put such a suggestion on paper, but no responsible government would think of it. At the worst crisis and in the worst misconduct of the Bank, no such plea has been thought of: in 1825 when its till was empty, in 1837 when it had to ask aid from the Bank of France, no such idea was suggested. By irresistible tradition the English Government was obliged to deposit its money in the money market and to deposit with this particular Bank.
>
> And this system has plain and grave evils.
>
> 1st. Because being created by state aid, it is more likely than a natural system to require state help.
>
> 2ndly. Because, being a *one*-reserve system, it reduces the spare cash of the Money Market to a smaller amount than any other system, and so makes that market more delicate. There being a less hoard to meet liabilities, any error in the management of that reserve has a proportionately greater effect.
>
> 3rdly. Because our *one* reserve is, by the necessity of its nature, given over to *one* board of directors, and we are therefore dependent on the wisdom of that one only, and cannot, as in most trades, strike an average of the wisdom and the folly, the discretion and indiscretion, of many competitors.

Bagehot's enthusiasm for the, safely hypothetical, natural system is engagingly naive, and ignores certain problems that would arise under such a system that he himself notes in other, more practical contexts. Thus, whereas he claims that in a "natural system" each bank would maintain sufficient reserves for safety, yet "the custody of very large sums in solid cash entails much care, and some cost; every one wishes to shift these upon others if he can do so without suffering. Accordingly, the other banks of London, having perfect confidence in the Bank of England, get that bank to keep their reserve for them." Is not the development of such centralization also a natural phenomenon?

Moreover the idea, put forward earlier in the quoted section on p. 276, that independent banks *would* lend freely in periods of crisis is contradicted by the practical experience of their actions during periods of crisis, (*Lombard Street*, p. 290): "At such moments [panics] all bankers are extremely anxious, and they try to strengthen themselves by every means in their power; they try to have as much money as it is possible at command; they augment their reserve as much as they can, and they place that reserve at the Bank of England." Also (*Lombard Street*, p. 57): "At the commencement of every panic, all persons under such liabilities try to supply themselves with the means of meeting those liabilities while they can. This causes a great demand for new loans. And so far from being able to meet it, the bankers who do not keep an extra reserve at that time borrow largely, or do not renew large loans—very likely do both."

Nor would Henry Thornton have approved of Bagehot's predilection for a system of independent banks maintaining their own separate reserves. Thus he wrote in *An Enquiry into the Nature and Effects of the Paper Credit of Great Britain* (p. 94) that

> it may be apprehended, also, that, if instead one national bank two or more should be instituted, each having a small capital; each would then exercise a separate judgment; each would trust in some measure to the chance of getting a supply of guineas from the other, and each would allow itself to pursue its own particular interest, instead of taking upon itself the superintendence of general credit, and seeking its own safety through the medium of the safety of the public; unless, indeed, we should suppose such a good understanding to subsist between them to make them act as if they were one body, and resemble, in many respects, one single institution.
>
> The accident of a failure in the means of making the cash payments of a country, though it is one against which there can be no security which is complete, seems, therefore, to be best provided against by the establishment of one principal bank.

Again: "If a rival institution to the Bank of England were established, both the power and the responsibility would be divided; and, through the additional temptation to exercise that liberality in lending, which it is the object of competition to promote, the London notes, and also the country bills and notes, would be more likely to become excessive. Our paper credit would, therefore, stand in every respect on a less safe foundation."

Moreover, the central position of the Bank results from its superior credit (not just from the advantages endowed by legislation); thus (p. 60): "The larger London payments are effected exclusively through the paper of the Bank of England; for the superiority of its credit is such, that, by common agreement among the bankers, whose practice, in this respect, almost invariably guides that of other persons, no note of a private house will pass in payment as a paper circulation in London."

Furthermore, the resulting correspondence system of interbank relationships leads to more prudent behavior, since country banks (p. 167) "... come under the eye of their respective correspondents, the London bankers; and, in some measure, likewise, of the Bank of England. The Bank of England restricts, according to its discretion, the credit given to the London banker. Thus a system of checks is established, which, though certainly very imperfect, answers many important purposes, and, in particular, opposes many impediments to wild speculation."

To conclude this section, both Bagehot and Thornton considered the question of banking system regime. Bagehot preferred a natural, laissez-faire system of banking *in theory*; both sought to reform the operations of the Bank of England in practice, on the grounds that a more fundamental change was not realistic politics. Thornton, on the other hand, saw the merits of a centralized, correspondent system, and argued against attempts to divide the responsibility for the stability of the system.

2. The Inherent Inflationary Tendencies of a Central Bank

Besides the general free trade argument for free banking, and for the abolition of Central Banks, a second general reason for a preference for free banking arises out of a distrust of government management of paper currency. Central Banks were generally set up initially in the eighteenth and nineteenth centuries to provide finance on beneficial, subsidized terms to the government of the day, and were often awarded in return with certain monopoly rights in note issu-ing.[3] This combination led, all too easily, to circumstances in which the Central Bank's notes would be made, at moments of crisis, inconvertible legal tender, in order to provide, in effect, the receipts from inflationary tax to the authorities. Distrust with paper cur-rency sprang primarily from such occasions: e.g., John Law's Banque Generale in France in 1716, the suspension of convertibility in the United Kingdom of the Bank of England, 1797–1819, and the issue of assignats by the Caisse d'Escompte in 1790.

It was not, of course, suggested that private banks should instead be granted the privilege of issuing legal tender, since the danger of allowing private commercial institutions to levy an inflation tax for their own private benefit has always been pretty obvious. The issues connected with the designation of bank notes as legal tender are quite complex, and it may be worthwhile to digress shortly to consider some of them.

With regard to the danger of allowing private commercial bank-ing institutions to issue legal tender notes, Bagehot, (*Lombard Street*, pp. 107–108) wrote, "A bank of issue, which need not pay its notes in cash, *has* a charmed life; it can lend what it wishes, and issue what it likes, with no fear of harm to itself, and with no substantial check but its own inclination. For nearly a quarter of a century, the Bank of England *was* such a bank, for all that time it *could* not be in any danger. And naturally the public mind was demoralised also," though he noted (on p. 167), "But the directors of the Bank with-stood the temptation; they did not issue their inconvertible notes extravagantly."

This was, Bagehot thought, largely due to the character of the Board of Bank Directors (p. 166):

> plain, sensible, prosperous English merchants; and they have both done and left undone what such a board might have been expected to do and not to do. Nobody could expect great attainments in economical science from such a board; laborious study is for the most part foreign to the habits of English merchants. Nor could we expect original views on banking, for banking is a special trade, and English merchants, as a body,

have had no experience in it. A 'board' can scarcely ever make improvements, for the policy of a board is determined by the opinions of the most numerous class of its members—its average members—and these are never prepared for sudden improvements. A board of upright and sensible merchants will always act accordingly to what it considers 'safe' principles.

Perhaps things really do change! Skeptics may wonder whether change is for the better!

For a very different perspective on the Bank's suspension, see Santoni (1984). Santoni argues that it was in the interests of the private-sector owners of the Bank to prevent inflation, partly because they were fixed-interest creditors of the government, partly because (p. 17) "the quantity of notes the Bank could issue was restricted by law to an amount less than or equal to the capital invested by stockholders." Accordingly Santoni sees the inflationary dangers as arising solely from the inflationary predilections of the government, dragging an unwilling private-sector Bank Court along under protest.

Even when private note issues are *not* legal tender, the issuers obtain seignorage, i.e., the margin between the rate of interest, generally zero (though see later—chapter 3) on the notes and the interest on the (default-free) assets held by the private note issuers against such note liabilities. Fama (1981) has argued that such seignorage is pure economic profit, and would, therefore, be a logical government confiscation in a world of taxation with positive deadweight losses. Such confiscation is, perhaps, most easily achieved by monopolizing the note issue in a Central Bank.

The actual importance of prescribing a currency as "legal tender" is, however, a tricky subject. Forcing someone to accept a particular currency in payment for some contract does not necessarily provide an advantage to the issuer of the currency if the terms, i.e., the value placed on the currency, of the transaction are left entirely free. It is the combination of the designation of a currency as legal tender, together with *fixing* its value in terms of some other asset, e.g., gold or another currency, that provides a clear incentive for overissue—see Klein (1974, pp. 431–432, 448). Even when the value of the legal tender currency is not, however, fixed by fiat in terms of some other asset, the inertia of prices, contracts, etc., may well provide an incentive for inflationary overissue—see Klein (1974, p. 436). Critics of Central Banks will immediately argue that such incentives may be similar, and even possibly worse, because of the short time horizon of governments, for public, as for private, note issuers.

Besides the example of the suspension of convertibility by the Bank of England, 1797–1819, there have been some other examples of the note issues of private banks being given legal tender status, at times when convertibility was suspended. It happened in Belgium, following the 1848 crisis, when "...the government, to prevent a greater crisis, allowed the Societe Generale and the Banque de Belgique to suspend specie payments, and gave their notes legal tender status." This experience cannot, however, have been regarded as satisfactory, since, immediately following the crisis, the authorities set up the Banque Nationale de Belgique with monopoly control of the note issue (details taken from Cameron, 1967, pp. 135–136).

The provision of legal tender status to the notes of a private bank in such circumstances, i.e., when convertibility has been suspended while the private bank continues in operation, may be differentiated from those cases in which the notes of a failing private bank of issue are guaranteed payment, in order to prevent panic, while convertibility may still be preserved. An example of the latter is provided by the failure of the Oriental Bank in 1884. It had provided quasi-Central Banking services in Ceylon, including most of the note issue. In order to prevent a financial panic and collapse, the governor, Sir Arthur Gordon, guaranteed full payment (in silver) of the failed bank's notes. In 1885 these notes were replaced by government notes issued by a Currency Board—see Gunasekera (1962, chapter 4).

During the course of the nineteenth century, the designation of the note issue of a Central Bank as "legal tender" was often, perhaps generally, an indication of monetary weakness, of the onset of the "cours force." Thus the notes of the Reichsbank and the Swiss National Bank (except at times of war) were *not* legal tender, whereas the notes of the banks of issue in Italy were legal tender, prior to

1909, but on several occasions, e.g., prior to 1881 and after 1893, "practically irredeemable"—see "Renewal of Reichsbank Charter," National Monetary Commission, (1910 article from *Frankfurter Zeitung*, pp. 43—44), and *Interviews on the Banking and Currency Systems* (Italy), National Monetary Commission (1910), interview with Canovai, Chief General Secretary of the Banca d'Italia, p. 513. The notes of the Bank of France were made legal tender on the crisis occasions, of 1848 and 1870, when it was forced to suspend convertibility: at that time the designation of notes as "legal tender" was virtually synonymous with "cours force"—see Liesse (1911).

As Pressnell has pointed out, in an unpublished comment, on a paper by Congdon (1981), designating the note issue of a bank "legal tender" "does not necessarily change the position that it will be acceptable only if sustained by real resources, e.g., by command over the economy through taxation, or by convertibility into gold or other currencies. Lacking such support, would not legal tender make a currency a *forced* currency?"

To revert, however, to the main theme of this section, the aim of most recent critics of Central Banks has been to prevent the development of a public monopolistic institution, such as the Central Bank, which might seek to manage the currency. It is, for example, Hayek's claim that "practically all governments of history have used their exclusive power to issue money in order to defraud and plunder the people."[4]

Clearly, acceptance of the case that the public authorities should undertake discretionary management of the note issue and the money stock would seem to entail the need for a Central Bank to undertake such operations. So, the case for free banking, without any Central Bank, must involve as a central plank an attack on the ability, or desirability, of such central "monopolistic" management; a good example of such an attack is to be found in Vera Smith's *The Rationale of Central Banking*, especially chapter XI, "The Arguments in Favour of Central Banking Reconsidered."

It is not, however, necessary to go so far as to abolish a Central Bank altogether in order to remove the authorities' ability to manage their own monetary system in a monopolistically discretionary fashion. The Central Bank may be constrained by various rules, e.g., to maintain a fixed exchange rate, e.g., with gold (the Gold Standard), or to maintain some preordained, e.g., constant, rate of growth of the money stock. This option, however, then poses a dilemma for a Central Bank whenever caught between the need to prevent a liquidity crisis in a fractional reserve banking system and the objective of maintaining the rule. Hayek, for example, has been of the opinion that, in such systems, there is a need for Central Banks, that such conflicts between alternative objectives could well occur, and that on such occasions the needs of the banking system would have to be paramount. Hayek's writings on this particular subject go back as far as his book *Monetary Nationalism and International Stability* (1937), where this issue is discussed in lecture V, "The Problems of a Really International Standard," especially pp. 76–84 and 88–92; the subject is taken up again in *The Constitution of Liberty* (1960), pp. 326–327 and 520. He returned to the subject in *Denationalisation of Money—the Argument Refined* (1978), in which (p. 96) he writes, "It is not to be denied that with the existing sort of division of responsibility between the issues of the basic money and those of a parasitic circulation based on it, central banks must, to prevent matters getting completely out of hand, try deliberately to forestall developments they can only influence but not directly control."

Consequently (p. 77): "As regards Professor Friedman's proposal of legal limit on the rate at which a monopolistic issuer of money was to be allowed to increase the quantity in circulation, I can only say that I would not like to see what would happen if under such a provision it ever became known that the amount of cash in circulation was approaching the upper limit and that therefore a need for increased liquidity could not be met."

Hayek did, therefore, see a practical need for a Central Bank within the banking system as it existed in practice.[5] Nevertheless, he became increasingly concerned (as the constraints on governmental misuse, as he saw it, of money fell away with the collapse of the Gold Standard, the rise of Keynesianism, and acceptance of deficit financing) with the risks that the existence of a monopolistic Central Bank provided to governments for excessive monetary expansion.

Initially Hayek thought that it might be sufficient, as a constraint on national overissues of money, to allow and to encourage competition between national currencies, e.g., by removing all exchange controls and allowing any contract to be legally conducted in any currency: "What is so dangerous and ought to be done away with is not governments' right to issue money but the exclusive right to do so and their power to force people to use it and to accept it at a particular price."[6]

Subsequently, however, he went on to propose the more radical step of allowing and encouraging private note issuers to compete.[7] This proposal was, in general, akin to the suggestions for "free banking," as considered earlier by Bagehot et al. in the nineteenth century. In such a system of "free banking" there would be no Central Bank[8] and no central reservoir of reserves: each individual bank would be responsible for keeping its own reserves, and the convertibility of its own, note and deposit, liabilities.[9]

The earlier proponents of "free banking," other than the simple expansionists, had envisaged banks issuing notes convertible into gold at a fixed rate, i.e., on a Gold Standard. Hayek's proposal is more radical than this. He would have note issuers compete in terms of the standard of value of the notes they offered, e.g., relating them to differing baskets of commodities. He thought that transactions and information costs could be reduced by modern electronic calculating machines, etc. Klein, (1974) also considers the possibility of banks offering liabilities, both notes and deposits, at flexible and varying exchange rates.

Assuming perfect and costless information, the liabilities of a more rapidly issuing, i.e., inflationary, bank could only be kept in circulation by the payment of higher interest rates. Klein relies on the need to maintain confidence and reputation, when information is less than perfect, to prevent accelerating overissue. In order to maintain such confidence, however, financial institutions (other than Central Banks) would have to be able to guarantee convertibility into some other asset: "In a strict sense, therefore, competitive costly information equilibrium implies that all money is at least partially 'commodity' money" (Klein, 1974, p. 438). There are also problems of paying interest on currency, costs of preventing counterfeiting, (Klein, 1974, p. 450), externalites of information, etc. On such externalities see Tullock's (1976) reply to Klein's comment (1976) on Tullock (1975).

Furthermore, the heterogeneous issue of individual banks could make counterfeiting more of a problem—see Cagan (1963, pp. 19–21) (in Carson, 1963)—though King (1983, pp. 134, 155) reports that contemporary discussions in New York in the free banking era did not stress this as an important feature of that system, and White (1984b, p. 40) also reports that "this was not a significant problem in the Scottish experience."

More recently, Hayek (1986) has despaired of the likelihood of achieving "denationalisation of the government moneys that are now used and their replacement by competing private currencies." Although this "would still seem to me desirable," yet it is "apparently wholly utopian since no government is likely to permit such a development in the foreseeable future" (p. 9). In this more pessimistic, but realistic, context Hayek has advocated the private provision of a medium of exchange and unit of account indexed to a basket of wholesale commodities, to be known as the *Standard*, which might initially be used primarily in international transactions.

There has been, indeed, a considerable revival of interest in proposals to relate the international value of the dollar to a basket of commodities, viz., Secretary of the Treasury Baker's reported interest in this idea, as expressed at the September 1987 IMF (International Monetary Fund) meeting. Then, if the fluctuations of other major currencies vis-à-vis the dollar were limited, their own international values would also be stabilized, by extension, against that same commodity basket. But there appear to be much stronger institutional and traditional barriers to the acceptability of alternative units of account and media of exchange, besides the official unit, within a single country, except in countries suffering serious inflation. So, alternative forms of indexed financial instruments have not made much headway, e.g., in serving as a means of payment in domestic transactions, even where their introduction is legally allowed—see my comments on Hayek's proposals (Goodhart, 1986).[10] Exactly why financial indexation has not proven more popular remains a puzzle that economists have yet to understand.

Be that as it may, the case for having a Central Bank certainly does get mixed up with the arguments for discretionary monetary management vs. rules, since discretionary management would seem to imply the existence of a Central Bank. Moreover, certain proponents of free banking (such as Vera Smith, who was a student of Hayek's at LSE—London School of Economics—and who later married Friedrich Lutz, an economist in the Austrian School) argue that the mere existence of a Central Bank, even if it normally follows certain rules of conduct, represents a standing temptation to the authorities to change the rules of the game and to debauch the currency.

Other advocates of free banking have, however, attacked Central Banks for being too conservative and restrictive, preventing competition and innovation by their regulatory restrictions. These critics would often have preferred the authorities to have encouraged a faster rate of money growth. Such critics formed, perhaps, the majority of the free banking advocates in the nineteenth century— see Smith, *The Rationale of Central Banking*—though White denies that this is true of the United Kingdom and the United States. A recent example of this school (though oddly ignorant of Smith's book) is Cameron (1967).

In any case, a major part of the criticism of Central Banks has sprung from dissatisfaction with their discretionary handling of monetary management, though such criticism has at times pointed to their innate deflationary bias (Keynes), as well as to their supposed inflationary bias (Hayek). Nevertheless in the rest of this book, I shall try to abstract from this issue, of rules vs. discretion, since it has been so widely discussed elsewhere.

If we exclude, by assumption, the desirability of having a Central Bank to undertake discretionary management of the note issue and money stock, the case for leaving banks then free to manage their own affairs rests on simple foundations. The claim is that a bank will attract additional depositors by establishing a reputation for maintaining, a fortiori for increasing, the value of its liabilities, whether notes or deposits. The locus classicus of this claim is to be found in Hayek's *Denationalisation of Money* (1976, pp. 40–45, 71–74). Hayek emphasizes (p. 74), "Money is the one thing competition would not make cheap, because its attractiveness rests on it preserving its 'dearness.'"

Per contra, a bank that loses reputation by inflationary/risky actions will lose the confidence and the deposits of potential customers, unless the bank offers depositors a rate of interest that (exactly) offsets the depreciation of its deposits (or note liabilities) relative to the most conservatively managed bank.[11] Thus Klein (1974, pp. 427–428) states that, under perfect information, "consumers are indifferent between monies of varying anticipated rates of price change and interest yields as long as the implied rental prices of monetary services from a unit of money is identical.... A condition of metastable equilibrium exists with regard to nominal magnitudes."

So, the natural pursuit of self-interest will lead to the transfer of funds to the prudently/conservatively managed:[12] natural market forces will, therefore, bring about a satisfactorily working banking system without outside interference or regulation.[13]

Chapter 3
The Key Role of the Clearinghouse

It is notable that discussion of information deficiencies and asymmetries, and of the possible role of insurance in such circumstances, which will generally feature prominently in any modern discussion of the need for (Central Bank) regulation/supervision over banks (and which will be further considered in chapters 5–7) did not play much of a role in the debates on free banking in the nineteenth century.[1] Instead, the discussion centered much more around the question of whether there were quasi-automatic market mechanisms that would restrain any attempt by a private banker to expand business excessively rapidly.

It was argued that, so long as an effective clearinghouse system operated, any single bank that expanded the size of its book more rapidly than the average would find its balance at the clearing becoming adverse, and would be forced to pay out legal tender reserves. This check on excessive expansion would operate whether the liabilities issued by the expanding bank against its increased loans were in the form of deposits or notes, though there was some presumption that the recipient of a bank check would be more likely to pay it in quickly to his own bank than would a recipient of a bank note, so the restraining process would work even quicker and more effectively on a bank with liabilities primarily in deposit form—see Smith, *The Rationale of Central Banking*, especially pp. 62–63, 86, 107, 157–162, 174–176. The earliest expression of these ideas in detail in the United Kingdom is to be found in Sir Henry Parnell's pamphlet (1827) "Observations on Paper Money, Banking and Overtrading, Including Those Parts of the Evidence Taken before the Committee of the House of Commons Which Explained the Scotch System of Banking."[2]

There are two flaws in this analysis. The first, which was considered at some length by Smith and the earlier economists engaged in the free-banking debate, is that the clearinghouse mechanism tends to lead all banks to expand, or to contract, at a broadly similar rate, but does not itself determine what the resulting average rate of growth might be, nor whether it would be stable, or subject to sharp fluctuations. The second, even more serious, flaw, as it now appears in a modern context, is that neither Smith nor apparently earlier economists had considered the possibility of more aggressive banks seeking to prevent the clearinghouse losses that would result from rapid expansion *by making their liabilities relatively more attractive*. Thus a bank, or any financial intermediary, aiming to achieve faster (than average) growth will tend to offer higher (than average) rates of interest, or other inducements, on deposits. That possibility would allow them to check the automatic mechanism of clearinghouse losses. Moreover, it places particular pressures on the informational requirements of ordinary depositors. If a bank, or other financial intermediary, is paying over-the-odds for deposits, is that because it is favored by greater efficiency or is undertaking a riskier strategy? In this context, and against the background of the earlier free-banking debates, it is easier to appreciate why the United States authorities reacted to bank failures in the 1930s by placing restraints on the payment of interest on bank deposits.

It may be argued that this problem, i.e., bank bidding for additional liabilities, does not apply in the case of notes, since these are noninterest bearing. But this need not necessarily be so. Bills of exchange were used to make payments in the United Kingdom in some regions outside London in the early part of the nineteenth century. In the event, despite the free-banking controversy, note issue in most countries was either unified in a monopoly bank of issue or heavily constrained in terms of requisite asset backing by the middle of the nineteenth century. If that had not happened, banks might have sought to have taken advantage of Gresham's law to keep their notes held outside for longer in hoards, by offering a premium (i.e., a rate of interest) if redeemed after some fixed date. They did so, indeed, in Scotland. Vaubel (1984a, p. 71, footnote 3) states that "until 1765, runs on the note-issuing banks were prevented by the so-called 'optional clause', first introduced by the Bank of Scotland in the 1730s. The clause, printed on the bank notes, gave the issuer the option of paying the bearer with interest at six months after sight rather than on demand. The optional clause was prohibited by Parliament in 1765." Also see King (1983, p. 155) for an account of the practice of issuing "post notes," i.e., issues payable at a fixed future date, either with or without explicit interest, in New York in the early 1800s. And Trivoli (1979, p. 10) reports that Boston banks issued interest-bearing notes for four years from 1825 to 1828: "... in an attempt to reduce the competition of country banks." His table on notes in circulation in Boston (table 1, p. 11) shows that such notes more than doubled during these years. There are several references in Cameron (1967) to the payment of interest on paper circulating as media of exchange; e.g., the use of bills of exchange in this role in England in the eighteenth and early nineteenth centuries, pp. 50–51; the optional clause in Scotland prior to 1765, pp. 68–70; the billets à ordre of the Caisse Generale in France in the mid-nineteenth century, p. 107; and in the chapter "Germany, 1815–1870" by Tilly, the account of the German system of bill currency, pp. 170–171. For a further reference to the interest-bearing sight bills of the Caisse Generale (1837–1847), see Liesse (1911, p. 74). In Sweden the national debt office in 1789 "created a new circulating medium in the shape of certificates bearing interest at 3 per cent, and of small face value"—see Flux (1911).

Be that as it may, an effectively working clearinghouse was seen in the earlier nineteenth century as an essential discipline on overissue—more important, perhaps, in this role than were the actions of the nascent central banks. It would be a mistake, however, to view the two institutions as alternatives. Instead, their roles became increasingly complementary. As a prime example, consider the history of the Suffolk bank system, as reported in Smith, *The Rationale of Central Banking* (p. 42); because of its relevance, it is reproduced in full below:

> A major deficiency over the whole of the American banking structure had long been the infrequency of the return of notes to their issuers. One of the earliest and most successful at-

tempts to secure that notes were redeemed more often was a voluntary system put into force by the Suffolk Bank of Massachusetts. Bank-notes circulated at places distant from their issuing bank at discounts varying with the difficulty of sending them home for redemption. The smaller was the chance of its notes being presented for payment, the larger was the volume of notes that a bank could safely issue. The result of the lack of any machinery for ensuring the collection of notes was therefore that banks began purposely to place themselves at long distances from the most important centres of business. This was what happened in Massachusetts. The banks of Boston found themselves at a distinct disadvantage because the country banks were securing practically the entire circulation even in Boston. Large numbers of country bank-notes never returned to the banks that had issued them, but remained in Boston circulating without hindrance at the recognised rate of discount. The Boston banks made several attempts to systemise the sending back of notes for redemption. The most successful was the Suffolk Bank system [started in 1819]. This bank arranged for New England country banks to keep with it permanent deposits of $5,000 plus a further sum sufficient to redeem notes reaching Boston. The Suffolk undertook to receive at par the notes of banks who made such deposits, and the notes of country banks who refused to come into the scheme would be sent back for redemption. The Suffolk Bank, moreover, refused admittance to its clearing agency to banks whose integrity was not above suspicion. This had the intended effect of curtailing the circulations of the country banks.

The point of this example is that the Suffolk bank, in furtherance of its actions to operate the clearing system effectively, was patently beginning to take on several of the functions of a proper Central Bank, e.g., acting as a bankers' bank and undertaking certain forms of supervision. For a longer account of the role and operations of the Suffolk Bank system, see Trivoli (1979), who describes the bank (pp. 18–19) as "...acting in some limited respects as a central bank for New England prior to the advent of the Bank of Mutual Redemption in 1858."

This "free enterprise" development of central banking functions was noted by Shenfield (1984) in his comment on Vaubel (1984a); thus he writes (p. 74): "It appears to me that this [history of the Suffolk Bank] merits fuller treatment, for it illustrates how a successful central banking system can emerge under entirely free conditions in which all transactions are voluntary." Also, see the account of this process in Salin (1984a, pp. 16–17). Salin accepts that there *will* be a natural evolution of central banking, but that privately developing central banks would probably limit themselves to "reinsurance" and not act as a "lender of last resort," the latter development not being "possible without public intervention." In my view this latter distinction is historically inaccurate and has no logical foundation. Also, see Timberlake (1984), who, describing the earlier history of US clearinghouses, wrote (p. 3) that "originally, one bank in the association was assigned the 'central' administration role for clearing the other member banks' accounts. Each bank kept part of its specie (and later, greenback) reserve as a deposit with this bank...."

In those cases where a bank was already of particular importance, e.g., owing to a privileged position as banker to the government and (monopolist) note issuer, it would be likely to play a dominant role in the clearing process. In countries with unit banks and country and regional banks, there would normally develop a tendency toward a correspondent system, with a centralization of interbank deposits.[3] Only in those cases where the banking system was, from the outset, based on a limited number of (oligopolistic) branching banks, all of whom could participate, more or less equally, in the main clearing centers, were such centripetal forces held at bay. The two main examples of this latter are Scotland and Canada.

Moreover, there are likely to be informational asymmetries between the knowledge that *nonbank* individuals have of the standing, strategy, and riskiness of the banks in any region/country/market, and the knowledge that *banks* have of *each other*. Transaction costs will ensure that, except for governments and the largest customers, individuals will only deal with a handful of banks. Banks, on the other hand, will be regularly dealing with a wide range of other banks and financial institutions. Competition should ensure that banks see what types of business are refused elsewhere, and what types of business that they had held are attracted elsewhere. Being in the business is bound to give banks a greater insight into the strategies, etc., pursued by other banks than can possibly be available to the general nonbank client, whether directly or from market signal. Insofar as the availability and accuracy of interbank knowledge about comparative banking status and behavior is much superior to that of nonbank individuals, it should follow that concentration of interbank deposits in those banks with the strongest standing and most prudent behavior is likely to be more pronounced than the ability of the general public to direct its funds to the same banks.

There are, of course, several reasons why a bank, especially a small, localized bank, would want to place interbank deposits with another larger, centralized bank. Such deposits generally provide a higher-earning form of holding liquid reserves than, say, holding gold, and, given the reputation of the large bank at the center, are just about as safe. The bank at the center can also provide various correspondent services and facilitate payments, participations, and introductions to the smaller local bank, and, perhaps, services (e.g., credit cards), to the local bank's clients that would not otherwise be available.[4] As Henry Thornton, *An Enquiry into the Nature and Effects of the Paper Credit of Great Britain*, put it (p. 155), "The creation of the large bank operates as a premium on the institution of the smaller."

The benefits of such correspondent features are well understood. My additional claim is that the informational advantages possessed by banks would be likely to lead to a concentration of such interbank balances among a few, central, well-established commercial banks, in some cases one or two banks. This would often happen naturally and would not require the prior existence of a Central Bank. This process occurred in the United States under the national banking system, 1863–1913, though it was encouraged and codified by the different treatment of reserves in the various classes of banks, i.e., country, reserve city, and central reserve city banks, established by the National Bank Act, 1863. Thus Smith, *The Rationale of Central Banking*, pp. 137–138, wrote, "The conspicuous position held by the banks of New York city in this respect—in 1912 six or seven of them held between about three-quarters of all the banks' balances—seemed to point to the existence of spontaneous tendencies to the pyramiding and centralisation of reserves and the natural development of a quasi-central banking agency, even if one is not superimposed." [5]

This process of natural centralization was given a further impetus in many countries by the need for the state to employ a bank to carry out certain financial functions for it, such as issuing notes, holding deposits, making payments, and arranging loans at home and abroad. In a few cases where the banking system was oligopolistic, as in Canada, or where a sizeable number of competitive large banks existed, as in the United States, the Treasury (in Canada the Department of Finance)[6] assumed some of these Central Banking functions itself prior to the establishment of the country's Central Bank. In many other countries, notably those in the British Commonwealth, the norm was for the state to use a leading locally chartered bank to carry out banking functions for it. This bank would then also undertake certain quasi-Central Banking roles. There are many examples: the trading banks established in the Australian States, such as the Bank of New South Wales, the Bank of Adelaide, and the Queensland National Bank;[7] the Bank of New Zealand;[8] the Imperial Bank of India;[9] the Bank of Ireland;[10] the Hong Kong and Shanghai Bank; and the Banco do Brazil—a whole list of others could be added. Not only did colonial governments require banking functions locally, but also they were regularly involved in financial transactions with the home country, for which they needed financial advice and assistance. Many of the British colonies used the London and Westminster Bank for this purpose toward the end of the nineteenth century, which provided quasi-Central Banking functions in London to the colonial governments. Thus I wrote (1972, p. 137), "The London and Westminster acted in many ways as a central bank for these colonies, providing loans and market advice, organizing their issues on the market, undertaking the paper work necessary, and keeping the books."

It is worthy of note that when such countries came to establish a Central Bank, they more often established an entirely new institution, started de novo, rather than attempting to build on the quasi-Central Banking functions already available in the leading commercial bank(s). Examples are to be found in the Reserve Bank of India, the Reserve Bank of New Zealand, the Central Bank of Ireland, and the Central Bank of Brazil. If full, legally recognized Central Banking functions had been grafted onto a large commercial banking business, it would mean, as argued further below, that an active competitor was being put in a position to regulate, supervise, and decide whether to support its rivals for business, which (I argue) would involve serious conflicts of interest.

A partial exception to this is to be found in the Commonwealth Bank of Australia. It was founded in 1911 more as a regular trading bank than as a Central Bank; e.g., note issue remained initially in the hands of the Federal Treasury.[11] It developed, however, further Central Banking functions during the interwar period, e.g., note issue, though Wilson describes its position in 1936 as "not strong," and "in September 1939 the Commonwealth Bank still lacked the powers of a fully-developed central bank."[12]

Nevertheless, in 1945, the Labour Government introduced an Act both "to strengthen the central banking functions of the Commonwealth Bank" and at the same time "to expand the Bank's ordinary banking business by active competition with trading banks, conducted in a department the accounts of which would be kept separate from those of the central bank proper."[12] Naturally this led to some concern, particularly among its competitors, since "a central bank must lose something in objectivity when it is a question of deciding advance policy for one or other of its own trading departments."[14] Yet it was not until 1960, with the founding of the Reserve Bank of Australia and its separation from the Commonwealth Bank Holding Company, that the standard division, between noncompetitive, non-profit-maximizing Central Bank and commercial banking, was finally introduced.

There are some further counterexamples to the normal tendency of countries to establish a Central Bank de novo rather than base it on an existing major commercial bank. Besides the Australian case, both the Central Banks of Egypt and Iran budded off from the main commercial banks of each country, the National Bank of Egypt and the Bank Melli, respectively. I am indebted to P. Edgeworth for this information.

Even where there is no impetus toward centralization arising from the needs of the state, the existence within the banking system of a part that is made up of small, largely independent units—even if the rest consists of institutions with large branch networks—will often lead these smaller units, often savings banks, to seek certain quasi-Central Banking functions within the system, often not from the ordained Central Bank but from a special institution set up for the purpose, such as the Central Trustee Savings Bank in the United Kingdom, or from a central commercial bank. An example of the latter occurred when the Dresdner Bank acted as a Central Bank to the Schulze-Delitsch savings banks in Germany at the end of the nineteenth century.[15,16] So there is a natural market process whereby banks, at least in any unit banking system, will tend to place deposits with another large, centralized, conservatively run commercial bank. This concentration of bank deposits with some central commercial bank(s), however, leads to certain problems becoming apparent.

In particular, the extent of centralization of reserves, and the provision of services, including insurance services, that will be utilized through interbank deposits between correspondent banks and a central *commercial* bank will be restricted through perceived conflicts of interest. The range of possible conflict between potential competitors in this respect is considerable. For example, it was stated earlier that one of the main functions of the clearinghouse was to maintain discipline on overissue by returning notes and deposits to issuing banks for redemption. Insofar as that function is carried out by one main bank, the conduct of that discipline may be seen by competitors as, and may indeed in some cases actually be, unfair, and certainly unwanted, competition. The opposition of such competitors, the state banks in the United States, was a chief reason for the successful political attacks on the First and Second Banks of the United States.[17] Thus Smith, *The Rationale of Central Banking*, pp. 37–40, argued (notably on p. 40) that "The chief objection brought by the latter [state banks] against the Bank was that it 'accumulated their notes and then presented them for redemption in coin'."

The same tensions arose between the Suffolk Bank in Boston and the country banks; thus Trivoli (1979), writes,

> Furthermore, the country banks had always objected to being forced to redeem their notes in Boston through the maintenance of deposits at the Suffolk Bank even though they enjoyed the advantage derived from the wide circulation of their notes at par. They had also objected to the restriction of the circulation of individual banks and the control over their activities possessed by the Suffolk Bank. The immediate reason for the final collapse of the system lay in the autocratic attitude of the Suffolk Bank toward the country banks, which was a natural but regrettable result of the unprecedented success of the system.

Insofar as the central commercial bank(s) is a competitor, other banks will be unhappy about placing deposits with it that increase the size of its book. This was a continuous concern of the London Clearing Banks in their dealings with the Bank of England in the late nineteenth century[18]—see, for example, Goodhart (1972, pp. 105–107). In a similar vein, Wilson (1952a, p. 220) reported that "initially, the Imperial Bank [of India] operated fairly successfully as a bankers' bank, holding balances for the other banks and even making advances to them. However, the fact that it also operated as a commercial bank had the effect of restricting the use that might have been made of it by the other banks, which were somewhat averse to seeking assistance from a competitor."

Moreover, there may always be, or it may be feared that there would be, a temptation for the central commercial banks to take the opportunity of a crisis to force a competitor out of business by *not* providing the loans/assistance that in more normal times a correspondent could have expected as a natural concomitant of the relationship. Since it is now argued that support/supervisory quasi-Central Banking activities may be provided by clearinghouses, rather than (or as well as) by dominant competitive commercial banks, it is as well to note that such commercial conflicts of interest may also exist in this latter case. Such conflicts appeared to play a part in the 1907 financial crisis occurring in New York—see Goodhart (1969, pp. 118/119).

Because the existence of such conflicts of interest is so important to the case for a natural need for a (noncompetitive, non-profit-maximizing) Central Bank, it may be worth documenting a number of examples of commercial rivalries between the central *commercial* bank(s) and its customers/ correspondents leading to some unwillingness of the central bank to lend.

The first example, taken from Thornton, *An Enquiry into the Nature and Effects of the Paper Credit of Great Britain* (p. 174), relates to the 1793 crisis. The centralized system placed much of the requirement for keeping the country's gold reserve on the Bank of England:

> Thus the country banker by no means bears his own burthen, while the Bank of England sustains a burthen which is not its own, and which we may naturally suppose that it does not very cheerfully endure. At the time of the distress of 1793, some great and opulent country banks applied to the Bank of England for aid, in the shape of discount, which was refused on account of their not offering approved London securities: some immediate and important failures were the consequence. The Bank of England was indisposed to extend its aid to houses in the country. The event, however, showed that the relief of the country was necessary to the solvency of the metropolis. A sense of the unfairness of the burden cast on the Bank by the large and sudden demands of the banking establishments in the country, probably contributed to produce an unwillingness to grant them relief.

The second example, reported by Vaubel, "Currency Competition in Monetary History" (1980 unpublished), concerns competition between the Bank of England and note-issuing joint-stock banks (outside the London area) in the 1830s. Vaubel writes (p. 4), "While initially 90 per cent of the newly founded joint-stock banks issued notes, this proportion decreased considerably when, in the second half of the 1830s, the Bank of England started to refuse to rediscount bills for joint-stock banks of issue and granted special facilities to those banks that handled its notes instead of their own." Also see Cameron (1967, p. 29—from whose work Vaubel was quoting). This example is given further point by Matthews (1954), who states (p. 196) that "it was this that was the immediate cause of the failure of the Northern and Central, for the refusal of the Bank of England in 1836 to discount bills bearing the endorsement of any joint-stock bank *of issue* [italics in original] made such bills unpopular in the London market unless their soundness was unquestionable." Also see an account in Matthews (1954, p. 178) of the Bank of England placing commercial pressures on other banks "... to abandon their own circulation."

The third example, taken from Bagehot, *Lombard Street* (pp. 280–282), pertains to relationships between the Bank of England and bill brokers in the years 1857/58:

> The Bank of England never deposits any money with the bill-brokers; in ordinary times it never derives any advantage from them. On the other hand, as the Bank carries on itself a large discount business, as it considers that it is itself competent to lend on all kinds of bills, the bill-brokers are its most formidable rivals. As they constantly give high rates for money it is necessary that they should undersell the Bank, and in ordinary times they do undersell it. But as the Bank of England alone keeps the final banking reserve, the bill-brokers of necessity have to resort to that final reserve; so that at every panic, and by the essential constitution of the Money Market, the Bank of England has to help, has to maintain in existence, the dealers, who never in return help the Bank at any time, but who are in ordinary times its closest competitors and its keenest rivals.
>
> It might be expected that such a state of things would cause much discontent at the Bank of England, and in matter of fact there has been much discussion about it, and much objection taken to it. After the panic of 1857, this was so especially.... Not unnaturally, the Bank thought it unreasonable that so

large an inroad upon their resources should be made by their rivals. In consequence, in 1858 they made a rule that they would only advance to the bill brokers at certain seasons of the year, when the public money is particularly large at the Bank, and that at other times any application for an advance should be considered exceptional, and dealt with accordingly. And the object of the regulation was officially stated to be "to make them keep their own reserve and not to be dependent on the Bank of England." As might be supposed, this rule was exceedingly unpopular with the brokers, and the greatest of them, Overend, Gurney and Co, resolved on a strange policy in the hope of abolishing it. They thought they could frighten the Bank of England and could show that if they were dependent on it, it was also dependent on them. They accordingly accumulated a large deposit at the Bank to the amount of £3,000,000, and then withdrew it all at once. But this policy had no effect, except that of exciting a distrust of "Overends": the credit of the Bank of England was not diminished; Overends had to return the money in a few days, and had the dissatisfaction of feeling that they had in vain attempted to assail the solid basis of every one's credit, and that everyone disliked them for doing so. But though this ill-conceived attempt failed as it deserved, the rule itself could not be maintained. The Bank does, in fact, at every period of pressure advance to the bill-brokers; the case may be considered "exceptional," but the advance is always made if the security offered is really good. However much the Bank may dislike to aid their rivals, yet they must aid them; at a crisis they feel that they would only be aggravating incipient demand, and be augmenting the probable pressure on themselves if they refused to do so.

The fourth example covers the relationship between the Banque de France and potential bank competitors in the mid-nineteenth century, as reported by Cameron (1967, chapter IV, "France, 1800–1870"). The Bank of France, apparently, used its influence to restrict competition from chartered banks. Thus "the Conseil d'Etat was loath to grant charters to banks because of the influence of the Bank of France" (p. 112; also see pp. 124–126). Moreover, when the Credit Mobilier, having been in operation since 1852, "in 1867, after it became involved in unsuccessful real estate speculation, its enemies in the Bank of France took advantage of its embarrassment to force it into liquidation." Also see Kindleberger (1984, pp. 279–280).

The fifth example comes from the events of the 1907 crisis in New York, reported by Goodhart (1969, pp. 118–119):

> However, the President of the Knickerbocker Trust Company, the third largest trust company in New York, with deposits of over $62 million, was also supposed to have certain (vague) business connections with Morse. On October 21 the National Bank of Commerce refused to clear for the Knicker-bocker, an action which under the circumstances could only result in a run on it. This action by the National Bank of Commerce is hard to explain. As far as can be ascertained, the Knickerbocker had neither asked for help nor really needed it, although it had suffered a succession of unfavorable clearing balances. Indeed, the Knickerbocker later easily (1) paid all its debts well in advance of the time set, (2) managed to have a large surplus left over, and (3) reorganised and began business again.[19] One suggestion is that this move was a part of the internecine fight then being waged in New York between national banks and trust companies.[20] It is possible that the National Bank of Commerce may have merely seized a convenient pretext to eliminate a rival, or rather a set of rivals; for the run on the Knickerbocker immediately turned into a stampede of depositors onto all the trust companies and eventually back onto the national banks themselves.

This was not, in fact, the last such extraordinary occurrence during the panic in New York. The clearinghouse committee forced four banks (related in one way or another to Morse), the Oriental, the Mechanics and Traders, the National Bank of North America, and the New Amsterdam National Bank, to suspend at the end of January 1908, although some of them could certainly have been saved, (see *Money Trust Investigation*, testimony of R. W. Jones, W. Sherer, W. Frew, and A. Barton Hepburn, especially).

A sixth example may be the refusal of trading New York banks to rescue the Bank of the United States in 1930—see Hirsch (1977, p. 247, footnote 10, and p. 250, footnote 12) and Friedman and Schwartz (1963, pp. 308–311).

In some large part, therefore, because of such conflicts of interest, so long as the quasi-Central Banking function is carried out by a bank, or banks, which sees itself, and/or is seen by its fellow commercial banks, as a competitor, then that function will only, and can only, be carried out to a limited extent. Distrust will limit the centralization and economies in reserve holding.

The provision of (lender of last resort) assistance at times of crisis will be made more uncertain and more difficult, particularly if it has to be arranged by a committee of major commercial banks with diverse interests. General control over the rate of expansion of credit will be made more problematic, if the major banks themselves have a separate individual concern for market share and profit maximization. A good example of this is to be found in the attempts of the independent Swiss banks to establish a uniform minimum discount rate in 1894, and again in 1898. In each case the refusal of some banks to join the agreement and its nonbinding character soon led to the "minimum" being undercut. A further example is provided by the Italian experience in 1885–1893, when commercial rivalries between the main banks of issue in the consortium of note issuing banks helped to fuel a ruinous, speculative expansion—see the appendix for details.

Despite the manifold problems of agreeing on common action, and how to share the (potential) costs of such support actions, historical experience suggests that groupings of major commercial banks—even in the absence of leadership from a Central Bank— can still on occasion mount partial support and relief operations during crises. Thus Timberlake (1984, pp. 13–14) wrote that a solution to banking instability was that "the banking industry simply reinstituted itself as an ad hoc central bank, and through its clearinghouse associations issued more currency." A more recent example that illustrates both the difficulties and the possibilities of collective commercial bank action is provided by the continuing debt crisis among some less developed countries (LDCs). Once again groupings of commercial banks, organized and guided by certain lead banks, have sought to develop a collective response. That collective response, in turn, has depended on guidance and leadership from the IMF in particular, but also from the Central Banks in the countries of those banks.

At times of financial crisis, the main commercial bank(s) will, on the one hand, desire to support their fellow banks, especially their own correspondents, not only because of a natural concern for their clients, but also because of a (possible) appreciation of the likelihood of contagion, whereby failures in one part of the system weaken the whole; on the other hand, the usual instinct of a commercial banker at a time of stress is to become more cautious, and less inclined to extend credit. Whether commercial banks, acting collusively, but without guidance from a Central Bank, could perform quasi-Central Bank functions depends on their number, the nature of the relationships between them, and the accidents of personality and leadership. It did happen on occasion: the history of the role of the New York clearinghouse banks in the various crises of the late nineteenth and early twentieth centuries is well retold by Timberlake (1984).

Nevertheless, and for obvious reasons, such quasi-Central Bank support operations are likely to be less effective, if done without the leadership and guidance of a noncompetitive Central Bank. Timberlake (1978, p. 190), reporting the arguments of Congressman Vreeland in favor of a Central Banking institution in the United States in a speech to Congress in 1911, writes,

> The present banking system, he thought, was analogous to a faulty railroad that would cease operations once every ten years. The dispersion of reserves in the present system, he argued, was an invitation to disaster. Five or six of the larger New York banks currently acted as a central bank, but their commercial nature—their profit motivation in particular— meant that they could not "afford to carry great reserves of from 40 to 60 percent when business is good, in order to release them when business is bad.... We must have an

institution to hold our reserves which is not a money-making institution. The idea of profit must be eliminated from its management."

Timberlake himself is largely silent on the possibility of, and the problems raised by, conflicts of interest between commercial competitors in his 1984 article. Timberlake would argue—I think, on the basis of private correspondence—that such conflicts would be less in the case of clearinghouse associations because these were trade associations and that their role was not to prevent individual banks from failing, but to prevent the contagion of panic from developing. In my own view, a trade association of commercial competitors retains considerable scope for conflicts of interest.

Relationships between keen competitors are always subject to pressure, and the diversity of interest among the competing banks is liable to limit support to its lowest common denominator. It is the *leadership*, rather than the direct financial assistance, provided by the Central Bank that has proved crucial in most actual cases of arranging such support operations. Like the IMF in dealing with the LDC debt crisis, in most serious cases of fragility in the domestic banking system, the Central Bank does not have sufficient resources itself to be able to deal with the crisis out of its own funds. Although the Central Bank will need to put some of its own funds "up front," to encourage the others and as a seal of approval for the exercise, the bulk of the funds will generally come from the (Central Bank inspired) collusive action among the other leading banks. This was how the Baring crisis of 1890 and the fringe banking crisis in 1973–1974, with the lifeboat, were handled, as was also the Continental Illinois crisis in 1984.

The crucial feature necessary to allow a Central Bank to carry out, in full, its various functions, e.g., of maintaining financial discipline, providing support at times of crisis, is that it should become above the competitive battle, a noncompetitive, non-profit-maximizing body.[21] This was not generally recognized at the outset. In the first half of the nineteenth century, the key feature of a Central Bank was seen to reside in its relationship with government and its privileged position as (monopolistic) note issuer: but in its banking function, it was often widely considered that it was, and should act as, just one competitive bank among many. This concept of a Central Bank's role was codified in the 1844 Bank of England Act.

But this was, as argued above, an incorrect, indeed faulty, concept, and, I would argue, true Central Banking did not develop until the need for the Central Banks to be noncompetitive had become realized and established. This metamorphosis occurred slowly and by trial, error, and debate in England in the last half of the nineteenth century, in some large part following the prompting of Bagehot. It was a difficult transition for two main reasons. First, it is not easy for an erstwhile profit-maximizing institution to turn itself voluntarily into a non-profit-maximizing body: existing investors (widows and children) may suffer in the process. Second, the assumption of responsibility for the health of the banking system that goes along with the move from competition to noncompetitive leadership was seen, notably by several Bank of England governors and directors, particularly by Hankey in his debate on the matter with Bagehot, as liable to produce moral hazard by weakening the self-reliance of the banks.

Bagehot's *Lombard Street* (1873) in chapter VIII records Hankey as stating, "The 'Economist' newspaper has put forth what in my opinion is the most mischievous doctrine ever broached in the monetary or banking world in this country; viz that it is the proper function of the Bank of England to keep money available at all times to supply the demands of bankers who have rendered their own assets unavailable. Until such a doctrine is repudiated by the banking interest, the difficulty of pursuing any sound principle of banking in London will be always very great." Until recently, Bagehot seemed clearly to have had the better of the argument with Hankey. Now that there is more criticism of official intervention and supervision in financial markets, and an understanding that Central Bank support operations make such supervision necessary, owing to such moral hazard problems, there is a greater appreciation of Hankey's argument.[22]

An account of how other European Central Banks developed in these respects is provided in the appendix.

Chapter 4
Bank Expansion and Fluctuation

As noted in chapter 3, the automatic loss (gain) of reserves through the clearinghouse mechanism accruing to relatively fast (slow) growing banks tended to force all banks to grow at around the same mean rate, but it provided no guide to what would determine the mean rate of growth, and whether that could be expected to be stable or unstable. There was considerable division in the historical debates on this topic. Some advocates of free banking, generally belonging to the Banking School, e.g., the Pereire brothers in France, were undoubted expansionists, seeing free banking as a means of holding down interest rates: there was often considerable confusion between the welfare advantages of introducing the institutions of banks and paper money into areas previously without them, and of having a faster rate of growth of bank liabilities. These advocates of free banking generally relied on the real bills doctrine, or "bankmassige" cover in the German discussions (see Smith, *The Rationale of Central Banking*, chapter VIII), to provide a satisfactory limit to bank expansion.

Not all proponents of free banking were expansionists, or from the Banking School (Smith, ibid., p. 127, provides a convenient tabular record of who stood where). The more conservative proponents of free banking argued that strict adherence to the Gold Standard, plus rigorous application of bankruptcy proceedings to any bank failing, for more than a short period, to maintain convertibility, would enforce conservative behavior. This was keenly disputed by the opponents of free banking. They argued that competitive pressures would drive the banks to seek to maintain and expand market share during normal (i.e., noncrisis) periods. Moreover, during such periods of normal business the more conservative banks would lose market share. With the public often being poorly informed, or incapable of discerning whether slower growth was due to conservative policies or lack of managerial effort and efficiency, there was no guarantee that the more conservative banks could recover during panics and bad times the market share lost in good times. These latter arguments were first stated in a quantified example by Mountifort Longfield (see Smith, ibid., pp. 74–76), an argument that Smith, herself an advocate of free banking, found "by far the most important controversial point in the theory of free banking."[1]

Insofar as competitive pressures did tend to lead to over-expansion during normal periods, it would lead to a drain of outside reserves (specie). When memories of previous crises had dimmed and all banks were suffering similar reductions, this might not of itself lead to more cautious behavior. There would clearly be a risk of a crisis occurring. At that point the individual interest of each commercial bank would be to draw in its horns and to restrict lending. Only collusive action, as discussed earlier, would be likely to remedy a crisis situation, and this would be improbable in a free banking context. The recent history of the rapid expansion of international bank lending to sovereign LDCs during the 1970s, the resulting crisis, and the subsequent cessation of further voluntary lending would appear to provide an excellent example of this syndrome. Competitive behavior seemed to force all the major banks to take part in an undue expansion of lending, and once the crisis broke, only collusive action allowed any continuing lending at all to take place. White, however, again analyzes these events from a contrary viewpoint. Thus, he argues (1983, p. 297), "Western banks would not have made such large loans to governments of less developed countries—loans that have been much in the news since their riskiness became manifest—had they not believed that an international lender of last resort, namely the International Monetary Fund, would absorb the risk."

My own reading of these recent events is that banks underestimated the riskiness of these loans, prior to the crisis in 1982, partly because of a belief that loans to sovereign borrowers were, ipso facto, secure, and partly out of a belief that diversification of loans

In any case, the argument that free banking is inherently unstable is *not* generally accepted. The advocates of free banking instead point, as prime exhibits of their case, to the examples of Scotland and Canada, where, despite the absence of a Central Bank in the nineteenth century, the banking system had remained generally robust.

There are, however, various reasons that may be advanced to explain the comparative success of the Scottish and Canadian banking systems. First, it may reflect in part the greater natural strength of a branch banking system (wider diversification, etc.) as compared with a unit banking system; thus Benston (1983, p. 10) records that in the United States "state-enacted legal restrictions on branching have had a negative effect on bank solvency. Almost all of the banks suspended in the 1920s and 1930s were unit banks: only 10 banks with more than two branches outside their home city failed during this period." Second, both systems became oligopolistic in form; in a smaller group of near equals competitive (and thus pro-cyclical) pressures *may* be less, though those who have studied the Scottish banking system (pre-1844) closely are sure that it exhibited high competitive pressures—notably Cameron (1967)[4] White (1984b), and Checkland (1975—though see pp. 272–273 for a partial acceptance of this point).

It may be worth noting at this juncture that the distinction between the ideal picture of free banking, e.g., as drawn by Bagehot, *Lombard Street* (see chapter 3), and the actual behavior of Scottish banks as reported by Cameron (1967) is considerable. In the ideal the individual banks were to maintain sizable individual reserves and to protect their reputation zealously. Cameron (1967, pp. 87–88 and 92) reports that Scottish Banks' specie reserves were minuscule—their main line of defense against cash drawings being their *own* unissued notes—and their accounting techniques were "casual." It is, however, clear that Scottish banks felt able to economize in some part on individual reserve holdings by being able to draw on London when necessary. Thus (p. 83), smaller provincial banks in Scotland held "a much smaller proportion [than larger Scottish banks] of their assets through London. Even that was largely for the purpose of maintaining liquid earning assets in

London in place of idle balances with other banks or cash in their own vaults." Earlier he noted (p. 81) that "... the great Edinburgh banks dealt more extensively in bills on London"—indeed, "... the exchange of notes and cheques between the Edinburgh banks is settled by a bill on London...." (Cameron, 1967, p. 87, quoting Thomas Kinnear). Also see Meltzer (1983, p. 108 and footnote 12). Probably the best authority on this topic is Checkland (1975); he writes (p. 432), "The principal and ultimate source of liquidity lay in London, and, in particular, in the Bank of England. This was especially so for the Scottish banks, which carried so little specie. The Bank of England had long known the burden that could be thrown upon it by Scottish liquidity needs. As one London banker had put it, 'Every banker in London is aware of a great drawing account in Scotland of several hundred thousands of pounds'." (Also see Checkland, 1975, pp. 433, 448.)

Thus, the final reason for the comparative success of these banking systems may reside in the improbability that under Gold Standard conditions either the Canadian or the Scottish banking systems could be said to be independent of New York and London. In both cases the Canadians[5] and Scots could relieve pressures on their reserves in their own areas by drawing on New York and London, thereby transferring the reserve pressure to the center. The Swiss also had a banking system without a Central Bank in the nineteenth century, with independent cantonal note-issuing banks. In practice, however, they relied on the Banque de France for support at times of difficulty and, when that was not available, e.g., in the 1870 Franco-Prussian War, the resulting adverse experience persuaded the Swiss that they needed a Central Bank of their own.

When these support facilities from the Banque de France were withdrawn, because of war or rumor of war, in 1870 and again in 1886, each individual Swiss bank ran for cover and tried to fortify its own position by restricting credit, thus precipitating a worse crisis. These experiences were influential in moulding opinion there for the need for a Central Bank—see Landmann (1911), especially pp. 13–15 and 83–86; also see in the appendix the section on Switzerland.

Although the centralization of reserves would transfer and concentrate the pressures at the center, the main Central Bank, or banks, could feel the same competitive incentives as any other bank. So long as such a bank remained competitive, it was difficult for it to act as a counterweight to the competitive cyclical forces driving the other banks. The easier problem was to learn to lend freely during crises: after all, this was at least being done at high rates of interest. As noted earlier, even still competitive groups of commercial banks could find it in their self-interest to provide quasi-Central Bank support at times of crisis.

The more serious problem of conflict of interest between the profit motive and the needs of the banking system comes not with panic (though policy failure may be more evident then), but in quieter periods. Assuming that the central commercial banks are trying to maintain convertibility into some legal tender, e.g., gold, their ability to do so, i.e., to allow their depositors and note holders to switch at par into such legal tender, depends on sufficient reserves of legal tender (e.g., gold) being held. With the correspondent banks economizing on their own liquidity/reserve holdings by holding deposits with the central (commercial) bank(s), this transfers the pressures to hold a sufficiency of reserves for the system as a whole on to the central bank(s).

It is not so much, therefore, the times of crisis and high interest rates as those of quiet and low interest rates that make the pressures of responsibility and profit conflict for central commercial banks. In Henry Thornton's *An Enquiry into the Nature and Effects of the Paper Credit of Great Britain* (1802), the whole of chapter VI is given up to discussing an analysis of this problem. If a sufficiency of reserves was to be held, the central bank would often have to sell earning assets in order to hold a responsible ratio (proportion) of nonearning reserve assets, just at the time when all the other commercial banks were expanding their own books.

So the central bank would either be forced to maintain insufficient reserves or be unable to maximize profits. This conflict of interest would be exacerbated insofar as other banks limited their own deposits with the central bank because of their jealousy of its "privileged" position—note well the dialogue between the Bank of England and the London clearing banks prior to 1913.

The ability of a Central Bank, or even a group of collusive main commercial bankers, to relieve banking panics by support operations is only half, and perhaps the less difficult half, of the exercise. The support operations themselves would, if expected to be successfully used in similar circumstances again, affect bank behavior generally, encouraging other banks to hold smaller reserves in normal times. Insofar as commercial banks acting together, as in the New York clearinghouse, could succeed in meeting panics by emergency issues of currency, there would be a resulting moral hazard, in that it might persuade other banks to hold even smaller holdings of available free reserves under normal circumstances. The dangers of inflation and the collapse of the monetary regime could then become greater. In order to be effective in controlling banking cycles, it is necessary for a Central Bank to supplement support action at times of crises with restrictive measures during periods of general optimism and expansion. The latter is extremely difficult, probably impossible, for a bank competitively seeking to maximize profits. The problems facing a still-commercial central public bank that attempts to carry out full Central Banking functions are nicely described by Timberlake (1978, p. 223):

> A bank panic or liquidity crisis immediately thrust the commercial-public institution into prominence because it had the only reserves that could save anyone and everyone. However, the institution's managers usually had little experience with or precedent for undertaking positive and sophisticated policies. In fact, what they had to do to offset panics and restrain crises was contrary to all their commercial banking instincts. As commercial bankers they confined loans, discounts, and advances to paper that promised a very low risk of default. In a bank crisis no such paper is available. The very nature of a crisis turns good paper, that is, short-term self-liquidating, bona fide loans, into highly questionable investments.
>
> In addition, a nineteenth-century quasi-central bank had to restrain itself during prosperous periods from lending on all good paper, which would have maximized its earning assets,

so that it would have some metallic reserves to parlay among commercial banks if they were threatened by liquidity drains. When a panic occurred, the now-central bank had to lean into the wind, and, as Bagehot prescribed, lend on what might be called subjunctive paper—paper that would be good when general business conditions were again normal. Thus the commercial-public-central bank had to be more conservative than its fellows during a boom, and radical to the point of foolhardy in a crisis! No wonder the directors of these institutions had such difficulty afterwards explaining their operations to governmental investigating committees. Central banking policies could never be rationalized by recourse to commercial banking principles.

Moreover, if a bank, or a group of banks, is going to assume responsibility for providing partial insurance against crisis, contagion, and general default, in circumstances where such insurance will in turn affect other banks' behavior (moral hazard), it is likely to seek to establish certain limits and regulations on banking behavior, in order to contain such moral hazard. The extent of supervision and monitoring involved can hardly be carried out on other banks by a competitor (see chapter 5). Once again, it is the noncompetitive aspect of the Central Bank that is crucial to the performance of its role.

Chapter 5

Information Inadequacy Leading to the Emergence of "Clubs"

Under some hypothetical circumstances, e.g., the public could obtain information correctly and costlessly, not only about each bank's current portfolio but also about each bank's future contingent plans for every possible state of the world, natural market forces would, indeed, enforce "good" banking behavior.[1] In practice, this requirement of perfect costless information does not hold.[2] For example, the ordinary individual will generally have neither the expertise nor the time to maintain a continuous assessment of the standing, riskiness, and reputation of the several alternative banks.

It was, however, soon realized that individuals were not likely to be able to obtain sufficient information to protect themselves in this way. In particular, the poor were seen as being at a disadvantage. The problems arising on this account in banking were nicely recorded by Henry Thornton, *An Enquiry into the Nature and Effects of the Paper Credit of Great Britain*, in 1802,[3] (pp. 172–173):

> Country bank notes, and especially the smaller ones, circulate, in a great measure, among people out of trade, and pass occasionally into the hands of persons of the lower class; a great proportion, therefore, of the holders of them, have few means of judging of the comparative credit of the several issuers, and are commonly almost as ready to take the paper of any one house calling itself a bank, as that of another. A certain degree of currency being thus given to inferior paper, even the man who doubts the ultimate solvency of the issuer is disposed to take it; for the time during which he intends to detain it is very short, and his responsibility will cease almost as soon as he shall have parted with it. Moreover, the amount

of each note is so small, that the risk seems, also, on that account, insignificant. The notes of the greater and of the smaller country banks, thus obtaining, in ordinary times, a nearly similar currency, they naturally fall at a season of alarm into almost equal discredit. If any one bank fails, a general run upon the neighbouring ones is apt to take place, which, if not checked in the beginning by pouring into the circulation a large quantity of gold, leads to very extensive mischief.

One consequence of this concern for the comparative inability of the poor to protect themselves, by enquiry into the relative credit worthiness of different bankers, was the commonly advocated constraint on the minimum denomination of bank notes, which was seen as having the prudential effect of restricting the poor to handling legal tender coins, thus avoiding their holding riskier bank liabilities.

Perhaps because of his confidence in the self-regulating characteristics of markets, Timberlake (1978, chapter 9) entirely misses the prudential aspects of this matter, and dismisses the proposed restrictions as just being erroneous prejudice. I would confidently expect, from private correspondence, that Timberlake would regard the prudential case for restricting small denomination bank notes as equally misguided. Why should one try to protect ill-informed, or poor, people from making poor choices about the goods that they buy, or the money that they choose to use? This is, of course, a large question, which cannot be answered here.

There was also a belief, probably justified, that small notes were less likely to be returned for redemption than large notes. Thus commercial banks wanting to expand fast would be tempted to issue small notes. Indeed, in Italy, prior to 1874, the issue of small notes was endemic: "The law of 1874 was intended especially to regulate the monetary situation in Italy because everybody was issuing 'notes', even individuals and commercial firms; the country was overrun with little notes of 50, 25, and 20 centimes issued by everyone who liked to do so" (*Interviews on the Banking and Currency Systems*, National Monetary Commission, 1910, interview with Canovai, chief general secretary of the Banca d'Italia, p. 516). There are many other quotes to this same effect in several countries to be found in the volumes of the National Monetary Commission.

On the other hand, the issue of small notes would economize, and allow the more economic centralization of metallic (gold) currency. While the advantages of this were clear, it was on occasions argued that this would make the Gold Standard less "pure"—see the article in the *Frankfurter Zeitung* in 1908, reproduced in *Renewal of Reichsbank Charter*, National Monetary Commission, 1910, p. 49.

Anyhow, the information base has not generally been, certainly not during the nineteenth century, sufficient to provide the transparency that might allow potential clients to observe accurately the risk/return opportunities involved in choosing between alternative financial intermediaries. The crucial problem is how difficult and costly it is for users of financial services to *distinguish* between banks with more, or less, risky strategies. If the deposits, or notes, of banks are effectively indistinguishable, then (as Klein, 1974, p. 429, and Friedman, 1959, p. 7, describe) there is an incentive for banks to overissue.

Klein (1974) argues (p. 430) that "indistinguishability of the output of competing firms will lead to product quality depreciation in *any* industry. In the money industry these problems are merely exaggerated." He holds out hope that investment in brand names by banks, thereby increasing confidence and reputation, might allow sufficient distinguishability to allow free, competitive banking (pp. 432–428). Also McMahon, deputy governor of the Bank of England, comments (1984, p. 48) that

> problems arise when it is inherently difficult for the individual consumer to assess the good or service he is buying ... there seems to be a case for laying down minimum standards or guidelines for some activities where an individual would find it hard to assess for himself the risk of loss in a particular transaction and where, at the same time, the cost of being wrong might be relatively severe. These criteria taken together might suggest ... a strong case [for serious supervision] in respect of life insurance business and banks.

Such information deficiencies would not matter greatly if bankers had low rates of time discount (and if their customers had long memories and an unforgiving temperament). Clearly over the long run a good reputation for maintaining the real value of clients' funds would be advantageous, i.e., would lead to increased deposits, and over the long run would be worth maintaining, so long as future returns were not heavily discounted. With a high rate of time discount, however—a short life but a happy one—a banker's objective would alter. It might be worth misusing established reputation, or developing a phoney reputation, in order to attempt to generate large immediate returns, without regard for longer-term returns, entailing a much riskier, go-for-broke, strategy—indeed, perhaps, in the limit a fraudulent strategy. Even if a bank had for years been run on the basis of a long-term conservative strategy, how could a potential depositor be sure that the bank's strategy might not change?

There is in banking a particularly serious free rider problem. With aspiring bankers having varying time rates of discount, those with the higher rates of time discount—greater propensity to assume risk—benefit from the reputations for conservative behavior established by their more cautious fellows. Owing to such informational constraints, "reputation," "name," "trust" are more important in financial intermediation than elsewhere: accordingly the free rider problem is also more acutely felt.

Thus, Hirsch (1977, pp. 252–253) writes, "As Arrow has emphasized, truth and trust are preconditions of well functioning markets; yet the habits of truth and trust cannot be expected to result from individual optimization, except perhaps in small and immobile communities where any benefit from transgressions is relinquished by the future costs imposed by the damage to reputation.... The non-market controls that permeate banking systems underpin efficient banking, as well as often undermining it."

Friedman presented a similar argument; (1959, pp. 6–7) he wrote

> What is involved is essentially the enforcement of contracts, if the failure of an issuer to fulfill his promise is in good faith, or the prevention of fraud, essentially of counterfeiting, if it is not. Both are functions that most liberals would wish the state to undertake. It so happens that the contracts in question are

particularly difficult to enforce and fraud peculiarly difficult to prevent. The very performance of its central function requires money to be generally acceptable and to pass from hand to hand. As a result, individuals may be led to enter into contracts with persons far removed in space and acquaintance, and a long period may elapse between the issue of a promise and the demand for its fulfilment. In fraud as in other activities, opportunities for profit are not likely to go unexploited. A fiduciary currency ostensibly convertible into the monetary commodity is therefore likely to be overissued from time to time and convertibility is likely to become impossible. Historically, this is what happened under so-called "free banking" in the United States and under similar circumstances in other countries. Moreover, the pervasive character of the monetary nexus means that the failure of an issuer to fulfil his promises to pay has important effects on persons other than either the issuer or those who entered into a contract with him in the first instance or those who hold his promises. One failure triggers others, and may give rise to widespread effects. These third-party effects give special urgency to the prevention of fraud in respect of promises to pay a monetary commodity and the enforcement of such contracts.

Moreover, there will usually be many clients, who, because of lack of information, greed, low risk aversion, etc., will be willing to invest in institutions offering over-the-odds for funds, despite potent signs of higher risks. While this trait may indeed deserve "caveat emptor," the greater subsequent frequency of failures will involve the informational problems that a bankruptcy/failure brings of distinguishing between those causes specific to the individual failure and those common to the set of similar institutions. Furthermore, the consequences of this difficulty of distinguishing between specific and general causes of failure can be much more severe in banking than in other areas. This is because the failure of banks causes people to seek to hold their liquid assets in currency, thereby precipitating a general run on bank reserves. The failure of an engineering company, for example, though it may embarrass its creditors, is unlikely to have secondary, "contagion," effects of the same order as a bank failure could and did, at least until some form of insurance was thought to be in operation.

Thus, in the CEA (Council of Economic Advisers) Report of 1984 (chapter 5, p. 147), it was stated that

> In the financial panics that occurred in the 1930s and earlier, however, depositors came to distrust banks; they withdrew funds and held them in the form of currency. One bank's deposit drain was not offset of another bank's deposit inflow. Because bank assets consist partly of cash reserves but mostly of loans to households and business, banks experiencing cash drains were forced to curtail lending, and perhaps to liquidate outstanding loans. As a result, borrowers were forced to scramble for funds. Business activity and employment fell, and interest rates on business and consumer borrowing often rose.
>
> As the business contractions continued, previously sound firms found that they could not service their debt, nor could unemployed workers pay theirs. Banks that had been unaffected by the developing crises found that their once sound loan portfolios had become shaky. Fearing more bank failures, depositors rushed to withdraw funds from those sound banks. As the downward pressures accumulated, the financial crises deepened.

Kareken (1981, p. 3) claimed that "... no rigorous and detailed argument has appeared in the literature," that "... bank failures have harmful third-party effects." By 1983, however, he (see Kareken, 1983) found such an argument in the article by Diamond and Dybvig (1983).

The arguments about whether bank failures are, or are *not*, more potentially damaging than the failures of other firms (of equal size) continue. Thus Kaufman (1987) argues the contrary case: that bank failures have not generally been more damaging, except where they have been such as to endanger the stability of the banking system as a whole. One of the major problems that Central Bankers face, however, is to be able to predict, ex ante, how far the failure of one bank will have spillover effects on the public's confidence in other banks, and thus threaten overall stability. Possibly Central Bankers' concerns about this are excessively acute: they may have been so, for example, in the recent Johnson-Matthey Bank case in the United Kingdom and with the Canadian Commercial Bank. But the greater moral hazard engendered by too hasty support *can* be restrained by more intensive supervision, requirement of higher required capital adequacy ratios, etc., whereas a collapse of any large sections of the banking system could cause untold damage. This subject will be further considered in chapter 7.

For the time being, we shall simply assume that the potential costs of large bank failures are considerable. As already argued, such failures derive in some large part from informational inadequacies. There are several potential responses to the problems thus caused by such deficiencies in information, which arise from difficulties in distinguishing between banks with more, or less, risky strategies, and between specific and general causes of banking failures.

Asymmetrical information, in which clients/customers know less than producers, is a characteristic—indeed, inherent—feature in the provision of specialized services, including not only banking and finance more generally, but also accountancy, law, professional agents of various funds, etc. It *must* be so, since what the professionals are selling is, in some large part, their own specialized knowledge. One response to such asymmetrical information conditions is to try to enhance the information base available to customers. Thus both buyers and sellers may find it profitable to increase the information available in the marketplace by paying for it to be provided. The role of advertising is obvious, as are its limitations from the viewpoint of a buyer wishing to obtain accurate and unbiased information about product quality. Buyers may be willing to pay for additional information from an independent testing agency. There are credit rating agencies and agencies that do provide specialist information on banks. The demand for the services of one such agency, Bruyette-Keefe, rose so much in the United States after the Continental Illinois debacle that the agency had to double its staff. Even so, when it is costly and difficult for anyone, even a specialist, to obtain such information, when the criteria for judging quality are subjective and uncertain, and when the form of the service crucially involves the nature of the personal relationships established, so that repeated searching is effectively ruled out (think of your doctor or lawyer), then the option of leaving the provision of information to the marketplace will often not be fully satisfactory.

This latter claim is challenged by some. Thus, Hayek stresses reputation as a stabilizing factor, as do several other economists of that view; reputation, however, also has a public good element, externalities relating to the reputation of others in the same field, that can easily be misused by free riders. Also, it is only too easy to appeal to the gullible by promising to offer a higher yield. Particularly when it is difficult to check directly and quickly the quality of the service, it is all too easy to persuade people that you have discovered a miracle cure. By the time that it is patently obvious that this is not so, the fake doctor may have obtained a large sum of money and moved on. In the field of banking, for example, it is extremely difficult to distinguish between a relatively high rate of return that is offered because of greater efficiency and one that is offered because the institution is also undertaking a much riskier strategy—for example, by investing in assets with a higher return but of lower general quality, such as "junk bonds." Because high return often is associated with high risk, it is notable that the rate of profitability in banking has *not* proved to be among the useful forward indicators of the likelihood of failures—for example in Z score exercises.[4] If people had infinite lives, and/or if memory did not decay, and if relationships between buyer and potential seller were capable of being repeated and repeated continuously, then reputation might, indeed, suffice to maintain the stability of the system. In practice, however, these conditions do not occur.

Moreover, in their infrequent dealings with professional advisers, e.g., doctors, lawyers, bankers, accountants, estate agents, and stockbrokers, clients are usually seeking advice and assistance about a matter that may have a major impact on their well-being and/or where a sizable proportion of their wealth is involved. It is much easier to rely on the doctrine of caveat emptor when the customer is almost as well informed as the supplier, when there are reasonable prospects of repeated purchases, so that reputation is important, and when the single transaction is not such that an inadvertent (or fraudulent or negligent) outcome would seriously affect the client's welfare. In contacts with professionals, clients seeking their services are naturally at an informational disadvantage, since professionals provide essentially specialist information, and so will often have only an occasional, or once-off, relationship, and may frequently have their well-being greatly affected by the advice and actions of the professionals.

Even so, the provision of accurate and up-to-date information on the financial condition of banks must play a major role in keeping bankers honest and up to the mark, and allowing customers a reasoned choice of alternative deposits for their savings. One result of financial crises has often been to induce the authorities to put pressure on the class of institutions involved to provide more/ better information; an example is Goschen's attempt, in the aftermath of the Baring crisis, to persuade banks in England to provide more frequent data on their balance sheet. More recently, following the failure of the Penn Square Bank, the FDIC (Federal Deposit Insurance Corporation) also recommended less secrecy about how banks—not as a group, but individually—were doing.[5]

It can be argued that recent improvements in the public availability of information on financial intermediaries, together with the existence of certain market experts—e.g., specialized analysts hired by Stock Exchange firms,[6] who are paid to report upon bank conditions—should allow developments in the conditions of individual banks to be quickly (and relatively costlessly to the ordinary individual) signaled in changes in their equity market prices. Thus it has been shown that equity prices of subsequently failing United States banks reacted rather quickly—indeed, in advance of the bank examination that led to their classification as "problem" banks—to the publication of operating and accounting data that earlier research had shown could be effectively used to discriminate between "healthy" and "problem" banks.[7]

Indeed, Goodman and Shaffer (1983) go so far as to claim (p. 3) that "competitive markets have been shown in theory to enforce disclosure of the optimal amount of information on which to base financial decisions, and indeed empirical studies have found strong evidence that the market generally reacts to a failing bank even in advance of its being so identified by examiners."[8]

Even so, it would still be costly in time and effort for individuals to monitor and to seek to interpret changes in the market value of all the alternative banks. Moreover, the exercise of shifting business from one bank to another is tiresome and costly, so that established bank depositors are, to a degree, locked into their existing banks. Differential costs of shifting funds and differential costs of information (even where there is no size limit to any insurance coverage) suggest that larger depositors (including other banks, on which more later) would be more likely to initiate a "run" than smaller depositors. As Benston (1983, p. 6) noted, "Bank deposits, particularly demand deposits, often cannot be diversified efficiently among several banks".

A statistical survey undertaken by the Inter-Bank Research Organisation (IBRO) in the United Kingdom in 1981 showed that 86% of current account holders in Great Britain had only one such account and that, despite changes in the population, job changes, retirements, etc., 58% of all current account holders had held their account for more than 10 years. This gives a clear indication of the extent of inertia—or the costs involved in shifting accounts from bank to bank. See Tiller (1982, p. II and exhibit 22). Also see Revell (1978, p. 51), who argues that "a major argument for opposing measures that would lead to more switching of customers from one bank to another lies in the hidden cost of switching a bank account. One of the main reasons for having a bank account at all is to have access to borrowing facilities when they are needed. Every time a personal customer switches from one bank to another, he loses the results of several years of painful building of creditworthiness in the eyes of his bank manager." This latter point is taken up further in chapter 7.

In any case, smaller banks will not, in general, have a market quotation, so there will be no regularly available, and published, indication to depositors of market opinion;[9] or, in some cases, the market will be too "narrow" or "managed" to provide a fair reflection.[10] In such cases individuals can make what (costly) use is possible of published accounts, statements, etc. The difficulties of obtaining a clear view not only of the present position but also of the future plans and prospects of any institution, including banks, remain manifest.

Under the circumstances in which information is inevitably limited, financial entrepreneurs may try to establish a reputation by more tangible methods,[11] e.g., the adoption of a high-sounding name and the use of a glossy office (The First Royal National City Bank of London or the Bank of the Western Hemisphere, to take two fictitious examples). I shall return later to the function of the supervisory authorities in limiting the accession by "free riders" to a spurious reputation by an "invalid" association of names and titles. Faced with "banks" possessing fine-sounding names, an imposing address, and a plausibly good-looking balance sheet, how is the individual to distinguish between banks that can offer a higher yield because they are more efficient and those that offer a higher yield because they are riskier? And, if a bank should default, how is the individual to assess whether the default arose from contingencies specific to that one bank or that would have a common effect on a group of banks?

Thus Korobow, Stuhr, and Martin (1977), report (p. 39) that

> One of the first tests of this nature [of management ability] made use of net income in relation to equity capital—that is the rate of return on investment—since we hypothesized that good management should be reflected in relatively high income. We found, however, that this variable can provide erroneous early warning signals since reported income cannot be adjusted for the riskiness of the underlying loan portfolio that generates the profit. Thus, a bank in the early stage of pursuing high-risk loans may show an impressive profit record only to report marked difficulty at a later date as many of the risky loans default. This was indeed the case when banks receiving low supervisory rating over the period studied often reported above-average income in the two or three years prior to the emergence of the difficulty.

Also see Barclay (1978, p. 3), who notes that "for example, suppose that one banker, A, is lending money which is certain to be returned at a rate of interest of 5% p.a. Another banker, B, lends money, which is 90% certain to be returned but has a 10% probability of being completely lost, at a rate of 6% p.a. Now, B is imprudent, by my definition. However, in nine cases out of ten, it will be the imprudent B who will do better than the prudent A."

Although there does, therefore, appear to be some evidence that the market can, and does, utilize publicly available information from bank accounts to discriminate rationally, by adjusting relative equity prices between sound banks and those that may become "problem" banks, it would be a long step to claim from this that (greater) provision of information, subject to the assessment of a rational and efficient market, will serve as a sufficient (or optimal) self-correcting market mechanism. As already noted, some banks will not have active, broad markets for their securities; and such market information will still be costly for individuals to acquire, to interpret, and to act upon. Moreover, as most studies of US banks failures report, these are generally caused by inept or fraudulent management.[12] Ineptitude may (should?) show up in the data; but dishonesty probably will not. Direct examination should help to deter, check, and uncover the latter (though even then will often not be successful).[13] Anyhow the apparent fact that markets can make some use of accounting data to discriminate to some extent between "sound" and "unsound" banks does not by itself imply that the extent of market adjustment is a sufficient, or optimal, guide for depositors or investors[14] (though, as always, more research on this subject would be desirable).

As already noted, such problems of informational inadequacy are not unique to banking, but occur quite commonly, notably in the provision of services, including other financial services. In particular, the difficulty, and cost and effort, involved in trying to distinguish between better, and worse, purveyors of a service is a common problem. It occurs, for example, with the choice, and use, of doctors, lawyers, teachers, stockbrokers, sellers of insurance, etc., etc., as well as with bankers. In all of these cases, there is a "free rider" problem, with those out to make a "fast buck" seeking to benefit from (and in the process to injure) the reputation of the more conservative.

No doubt because the problem is a common one, there is also a common response, which is to form a club of members providing the service in question, with (quality) controls on entry and rules of conduct for continuing membership. There are important differences in the extent to which the "professional" clubs are self-regulated, or are regulated by statutory bodies, or by government departments, differences that have yet to be adequately analyzed by economists. Nevertheless, there are some common functions carried out by, say, the British Medical Association, the Stock Exchange Council, the Bar Council, the Registrar of Friendly Societies, the Bank of England, etc., etc., which are necessitated by these common (primarily informational inadequacy) problems. Indeed, several other such regulatory bodies provide a degree of insurance to customers of club members, e.g., in the form of compensation funds, as organized by the Stock Exchange, ABTA, Law Society, etc. To this extent, it can be argued that there is nothing particularly special about the regulatory and supervisory functions of the Central Bank within the banking system.

Indeed, an alternative way of looking at the role of a Central Bank is to set this within the context of a banking club. Because of the cost and other difficulties of obtaining and disseminating information, the reputation and trust attaining to any one bank (financial intermediary) is closely intertwined (with causality running in both directions) with the reputation, etc., of the group of banks as a whole. This means that an interloper, which can plausibly purport to be one of the group, can benefit from existing reputations in order to obtain deposits. Moreover, the pursuit of a high return/high risk strategy, whether by an interloper or by an existing member, is made more attractive insofar as more of the costs, of future loss of reputation, are more widely spread.

A solution to the free rider problem is to form a club, which will keep out "undesirables" and will also have club regulations that will induce members to behave in a way that will benefit the membership as a whole. Thus, Klein (1974, p. 447) notes that

> Given declining costs of supplying information, a single firm or private trade association would be efficient in producing

confidence for a group of monies. The monopolistic or co-operative association could provide a dominant money and implicit or explicit insurance to consumers of member firms, similar to the use of warranties for other durable goods. However, such an arrangement increases distinguishability costs and therefore the incentive for individual member firms to overissue and consume the brand-name capital of other firms in the association. The association would therefore have to assume some control over member firm production decisions to internalize what would otherwise be unheeded externalities. If any firm in the money industry can take advantage of general consumer confidence and significantly damage the reputation of other producers, the economic forces for compulsory membership and highly regulated or monopolistic organization will be magnified.

Also, see McMahon (1984, p. 48), who states that

... personal knowledge could—and can—be further extended by the development of a club or market, membership of which would only be granted to those who were believed on direct evidence to be trustworthy—and which, once granted, provided a form of encapsulated information for others who had no direct knowledge of the man concerned.

For small markets this form of information dispersal may well be the most effective; as it can also provide the most effective basis for supervision by an outside authority. It had traditionally formed the basis of the Bank of England's supervision of the British banking system; and though in this case the vast increase in the number of people and institutions involved in banking has required that it be supplemented by more formal information requirements, we still regard knowledge of the people concerned as the most important supervisory tool.

To take this approach a step further, the supervisor himself may be seen as an efficient way of encapsulating some of the information necessary for the market concerned to work. He may do this partly by requiring particular forms of public transparency; but it may be at some points more efficient for him simply to make his own judgements on the basis of qualitative assessments which he then transfers to the markets in the form of a seal of approval, a licence or a recognition.

In the case of professional and business "clubs," however, there can often be a problem; if the club officials are to be drawn from the ranks of the competing, commercial members, there is the possibility of a conflict of interest. Indeed, it is notable that there was continuous and severe friction and frequent antagonism between the other commercial banks and the Central Bank so long as the latter remained a competitor. The rival commercial banks often tried to restrict, even abolish, the Central Bank's role.

Moreover, where control is left in the hands of the ordinary commercial members of the club, limits on new entry may be so tightly drawn as to restrain competition unduly. The club regulations may be drawn up so as to benefit unfairly those institutions currently in charge of the key club committees. Furthermore, it may well be impossible to check whether club members are obeying the regulations without spot checks, close monitoring, etc., which would be intolerable between competing members.

In cases where such conflicts of interest are less marked and less obvious, the club can be run by electing certain of its own members to run the club. This happens, for example, with the medical profession, the Stock Exchange, and many other professional bodies. In cases where conflicts of interest are more acute, as in the case of the banking system, or are perceived to have become more acute, as in the case of Lloyds Insurance, such conflicts make the operation and direction of a club by its own members more problematic and subject to abuse.

One obvious solution to this problem is to appoint an *independent* arbiter as club president, secretary, etc., who is *not* involved in the competitive, commercial enterprise of the members. The independent arbiter then both sets the boundary line for entry into the club and monitors and enforces the club rules. Because they cannot otherwise cope with the free rider problem without running up against conflict of interest, this development is greatly in the interests of the members of the club—in this case, the banks. Accordingly, once it was established that Central Banks were to be noncompetitive, their foundation has generally been supported by the banks, certainly by the larger, well-established banks, in the countries involved.

Sandler and Tschirhart (1980) state (p. 1497) that "privately owned clubs must be operated by a firm rather than by its members if free rider problems with respect to the goods' maintenance are to be avoided." In this case the impure public good, in the terminology of the theory of clubs, is the public's confidence in the good reputation of banks. They also note (pp. 1491–1492) that "in heterogeneous clubs [where members are not identical], members' goals differ, which can necessitate a centralized authority to enforce decisions and to determine memberships."

Whether the voluntary adoption of (self-) regulation, operated by an independent arbiter, can be maintained depends in some large part on the cohesion of the club members, which in turn depends, inter alia, on the number of club members and on the complexity of the activities of the club members.[15] When the number is large and/or cohesion is lost for other reasons, it will become progressively harder to maintain voluntary self-regulation. In such cases the achievement of the objectives of regulation, e.g., overcoming the free rider problem and provision of insurance, can only be obtained by a greater resort to legal powers and officially instituted bodies. As Sandler and Tschirhart (1980) report (p. 1497), "myriad institutional forms exist for clubs." Like many other economists they are, however, suspicious of "government-operated ones owing to short-run political objectives."

As many others have commented, the establishment of a public body, which is, however, separated from, and independent of, the immediate political arena, can be regarded as a means of seeking to achieve results that private action cannot, because of conflicts of interest and lack of cohesion among members, without running into the disadvantages of short-run political manipulation. Whether the constitutions of Central Banks are well designed for that purpose is debatable.

To recapitulate, the free rider problem, in conditions where the contagion of distrust is particularly likely and dangerous, makes regulation in the interests of existing banks. The natural process of centralization of interbank deposits with leading commercial banks tends toward the development of a banks' club. Conflicts of interest between banks, however, lessen the use and effectiveness of such pure self-regulation. The choice between a voluntary club with an independent arbiter and a legally imposed set of rules with an official body, or bodies, to run the system depends on the number and cohesion of the members.

Although, on paper, the distinction between these latter two alternatives seems considerable, in practice the differences are often blurred. Moreover Hirsch (1977), who described these two alternative approaches, argues that the effects on the banking system may be similar in either case. Thus the voluntary club approach involves cartels. Under the more legalistic approach, the regulatory bodies will feel some need to allow badly run banks to collapse, in order to avoid moral hazard, but will come under pressure to support larger banks in order to avoid system crises. So, there will be some natural tendency for depositors to regard large banks as safer. The shift of deposits to larger banks would then lead toward oligopoly (Hirsch, 1977, p. 252).

This tendency toward oligopoly can, however, be averted by some combination of insurance, for smaller depositors at least, and separate legal constraints on banks' expansion (e.g., the McFadden Act). Whether an oligopolistic banking system would be more, or less, efficient and innovative than one that remains fragmented because of the existence of legal constraints on competition from larger banks is a subject beyond the confines of this study.

So the presence of an independent, noncompetitive Central Bank is likely to be welcomed by other banks, at least by the larger banks with a reputation to defend. The transition of the Bank of England, from a profit-maximizing, competitive bank to such a fuller role, did occur naturally, but it was not an easy passage. The historical development of other European Central Basks in this respect in the latter part of the nineteenth century is described in the appendix. Outside Europe, most other Central Banks were set up by legislation as non-profit-maximizing, noncompetitive, ab initio. Even despite the conformity of interest between the Central and the commercial banks, points of friction, however, are bound to remain. Good, effective club officials are not cheap to maintain. So how is their cost distributed among the members?[16] Where the Central Bank obtains, in some countries, the returns from seignorage, or in others is a public sector body supported in all, or in part, by taxpayers, this problem is less acute. On the other hand, when the Central Bank is *not* financed by member banks, the issue of the responsiveness of the Central Bank to members' concerns becomes more pressing.[17]

In those cases where an independently appointed club official is dealing with a notably rich, powerful, and long-standing club member, one of the founding fathers, then, whatever the rules may indicate formally, the club official is bound to proceed carefully and cautiously. One of the more delicate and esoteric aspects of behavior in the operation of any club involves the attempt to limit and overcome points of direct friction in the working of such a club between its independent officials and key members.

Clearly, when the independent club arbiter, in this case the Central Bank, is trying to apply the agreed rules of the club in individual cases, whether institution X is fit to join the club and call itself a bank, whether institution Y is behaving sufficiently prudently (e.g., in maintaining agreed capital or liquidity ratios), then there can hardly be any objection, or appeal, against the independent arbiter, except on legal grounds as to whether it has interpreted the agreed rules correctly. In a number of countries, however, the bodies that act as independent arbiters of conditions of entry, and of rules of behavior, for banks are separated from the Central Bank—e.g., the United States, Canada, and West Germany. But in all such cases these other bodies work very closely with the Central Bank. I would argue that, although formal separation is clearly possible, these functions are an inherent part of Central Banking, and that oversight of prudential conditions in banking and the conduct of monetary policy in the macro context are closely interrelated. Moreover, as Benston (1983) notes (pp. 14–16), a multiplicity of separate, but overlapping, supervisory agencies (p. 16) "... can lead to conflicting authority and a failure to act in a timely fashion." And Revell (1975,

p. 37) claims that "one of the main criticisms to be applied to the American system of prudential regulation is the multiplicity of supervisory agencies, each with its own methods.... It is difficult to see how differences in basic approach between supervisory agencies can be justified; the only way to avoid them seems to be the amalgamation of the various agencies." An advocate of laissez-faire banking, Kareken, noted (1981, p. 4), however, that "a multiplicity of regulatory agencies may afford banks needed protection from government." Moreover, Edward Kane (1984, p. 4) argues that since "... agency heads seldom hold office very long, the desire to conduct a trouble-free watch imparts a myopically overregulatory bias to agency decision making." Consequently: "... in the long run, competition among financial regulators lowers the level of the regulatory tax by fostering efficiency in the production of regulatory services." In particular: "Regulated firms (especially new entrants into regulated and substitute markets) shrink the domains (and therefore the budget resources) of regulators whose response to the evolving needs of the marketplace proves shortsighted or inflexible."

Even more complex considerations arise when the issue at stake is not the implementation of the existing rule book, but the promulgation of new, or revised, rules. Then the question arises of the relative roles of the club members (the banks), the club officials (the Central Bank), and other interest groups (notably the Treasury and government). Which of these plays the key role in introducing proposals for change, and how far does each need to be consulted and agree with the proposal before the change can be implemented? These are difficult questions: the answer appears to change over time and between countries.

Chapter 6

Private Insurance?

In the nineteenth century, the advocates of free banking argued that the banking system could be trusted to operate effectively without external constraints or regulation, except in the form of limitations on what could serve as legal tender, e.g., specie, and the rigorous enforcement of bankruptcy for failing to maintain convertibility. Despite the record of the Scottish and Canadian banks, experience suggested that competitive pressures in a milieu of limited information (and, thence, contagion risks) would lead to procyclical fluctuations punctuated by banking panics. It was this experience that led to the formation of noncompetitive, non-profit-maximizing Central Banks.

Those critical of Central Banks, however, contend that their formation led to various forms of moral hazard. Thus their existence offered temptation to governments to misuse the ability to create money and impose an undemocratic inflation tax, and a temptation to officials to seek to undertake discretionary management that they had not the competence to attempt. But if then the Central Bank was to be abolished, or severely restricted in its operations by rules, how would its support and insurance functions, to contain contagious crises, be undertaken?

The answer that is sometimes given to this, though often without much conviction or enthusiasm, is that this could be provided by the banks combining to set up private insurance of deposits. It is argued that this could be done, because it would be in the interests of the banks themselves.

It is, however, notable that, whereas the support functions of Central Banks did evolve naturally (e.g., these functions were not only *not* imposed in the 1844 Bank of England Act, but the banking paradigm codified there was actually antipathetic to the subsequent development of central banking in England), there have been relatively few examples of private measures to adopt insurance among deposit-taking institutions.

Benston (1983, pp. 8–9) reports that there were some deposit guarantee systems organized in certain states by "mutual agreement among participating banks." Such systems were established in Indiana (1834), Ohio (1845), and Iowa (1858): "They operated successfully, largely because they empowered system officials to monitor operations of the participating banks and to control excessive risk-taking. Yet a second wave of deposit guarantee plans for states proved less successful. With one exception (Mississippi), the plans did not include effective supervision and they failed. These included … the voluntary plans of Kansas (1909), Texas (1910), and Washington (1917)." McCarthy (1980) notes (p. 580) a 1933 publication by the American Bankers Association, which concluded that "… these historical experiences show that the guaranty plan is inherently fallacious and based on erroneous premises and assumptions."

Instead, most instances of deposit insurance have generally either been imposed by external legislation or adopted under moral suasion from the authorities. Thus, McCarthy (1980) reports (p. 544) that "in practice, most of the deposit insurance schemes presently in existence have been organized, and to some extent imposed, by the monetary authorities, and in some schemes participation in the administration of the scheme is expressly forbidden to private bankers." Again, the Green Paper on Building Societies issued by the British Government, *Building Societies: A New Framework*, Cmnd 9316 (London: HMSO, 1984), states (chapter 5, paragraphs 31–32), "The present Building Societies Investor Protection Scheme, sponsored by the Building Societies Association but not confined to its members is a voluntary one…. The Association said when they introduced this Scheme that it was a stop-gap until there was a legislative one. The Government agree that there should be legislative provision for such a scheme, to which all societies have to contribute." Some of the problems involved in setting up a private insurance scheme are well illustrated by the difficulties and complexities involved in persuading the banks in the United Kingdom to set up such a scheme—on which see Moran (1984, especially pp. 125–130).[1] A major problem was how to allocate, and to limit, the costs involved. The larger branch banks argued that their position made them naturally more secure, so that to share the costs simply on the basis of the volume of (insured) deposits in each bank would mean that they would be subsidizing their weaker, but more aggressively competitive, brethren. Moreover, such insurance would make investors happier to shift funds to higher risk/higher return competitors.

There is no objective, and widely agreed, means of assessing risk. Without such, any methods of apportioning the costs, setting premiums for insurance, is not only bound to be contentious, but will cause dissension and disagreement among the participating banks. Moreover, if the insurance agency is to limit moral hazard, without being able to relate the premiums objectively to the risk, it will want to be able to conduct supervision and impose regulations on bank behavior of a kind exactly similar to those already being carried out by a Central Bank.[2]

Consider, for example, chapter 5, "Financial Market Deregulation" (e.g., p. 165), in the 1984 CEA report (Council of Economic Advisers, 1984):[3]

> Currently, the premiums charged by the FDIC and FSLIC are proportional to the amount of assessable deposits regardless of the riskiness of the intermediary's assets. Under this system, insured institutions have an incentive to take on more risk than they would otherwise, either by making riskier loans or by increasing leverage. Doing so does not subject them to higher premiums, and they obtain the benefits of the higher yields that normally accompany the assumption of greater risk.
>
> With the premiums unrelated to risk, therefore, regulation of insured intermediaries is justified. It is not coincidental that many restrictions on competition accompanied the introduction of deposit insurance in the Banking Act of 1933. In fact, the primary thrust of financial legislation through the 1930s, much of which is still in place, was to supplant or limit com-

petition in the market for financial services, both to prevent bank failures and to protect the assets of the insuring agencies.

See also Goodman and Shaffer (1983); they review a number of problems inherent in trying to relate such insurance premiums to measured risk (pp. 11–15), notably that such measurements will generally fail to cope adequately with new, and previously unanticipated, sources of risk, so that "like the dog chasing its own tail, a risk-based premium would thus find itself always playing catchup, in the process driving its goal ever more swiftly just beyond its reach" (p. 14).

In any case, variable insurance premiums may not necessarily remove the moral hazard problem. Thus Guttentag and Herring (1982a) argue (p. 120) that "variable insurance premiums would be even less effective in controlling the risk exposure of an insolvent firm under insurer control than they would be in influencing a problem firm before insolvency...." This subject has recently been treated at much greater length by Kane (1985).

If the insurance cover to be provided by, say, the private sector were 100% complete, the moral hazard would then be even greater than under current arrangements, so the extent of control and regulation might well have to be even greater than at present. These regulations, and such supervision, would no doubt on occasion be resented. How would a *private* insurance body be able to enforce its authority over its members without official and legal support? It could threaten to remove the insurance cover, but that might often seem too drastic a step. The danger of a private insurance agency being "captured" by its major clients *may* well be greater than in the case of a public agency.

If the insurance cover were less than 100%, the insurance agency might still face the possibility of runs and contagion. Indeed, even with full 100% cover, the administrative complications and temporary embarrassment and illiquidity faced by depositors in a failing bank could still cause "runs." Moreover, even if runs were successfully prevented, there could still be systemic problems, if major groups of banks ran into serious bad-debt problems that could imperil the solvency of the insurance agency itself.

Thus the safety fund for New York chartered banks in the early nineteenth century, set up under the Safety Fund Act of New York State, effectively became insolvent itself in 1845, and "... the legislature authorized an issue of state bonds, secured by the future payments from the safety fund, to pay the creditors of insolvent banks," and no further insurance payments were permitted from the fund until that debt was paid off—see King (1983, p. 149 especially).

This same problem was exemplified recently by the inability of private insurance to meet losses in the face of runs on S&Ls (Savings & Loans) in Ohio and Maryland, leading to a major shift of S&Ls to join the public-sector-run FSLIC (Federal Savings and Loans Insurance Coporation). Indeed, the failure of just one large S&L in Ohio was sufficient to exhaust the reserves of the private insurance agency.

In order to deal with these systemic problems, it would seem necessary for some public institution to stand behind any private insurance system, and to be seen to be ready, if necessary, to inject additional money into it.[4] But if so, the public authorities would then, presumably, wish to oversee the strategic deliberations of the private system. Moreover, the probability of serious, contagious (bank) failures is, presumably, quite low, but the potential costs of dealing with such a (rare) contingency could be very high. In order to maintain credibility, a private insurance scheme would need to maintain continuously large, visible reserves, which would be costly. A government sponsored insurance scheme could rely on the authorities' powers to create money and levy taxes ex post facto. As Diamond and Dybvig (1983), note (p. 416), "Because insurance companies do not have the power of taxation, they must hold reserves to make their promise credible. This illustrates a reason why the government may have a natural advantage in providing deposit insurance."

The end result, therefore, of an attempt to provide such general deposit insurance would probably be to establish an institution whose role and function would not essentially differ greatly from the supervisory departments in existing Central Banks, or the specially established separate public regulatory bodies that supervise banks.

Such problems have led to the consideration whether private deposit insurance might be better targeted at more limited, partial objectives. Thus, if the purpose of the insurance scheme is more limited—in particular, if the objective is not to deter runs on banks but, instead, to protect (a proportion of) the holdings of small depositors in failing banks—then the case for privately organized and financed insurance is stronger. Indeed, the existence of such limited private insurance might allow the authorities to accept the prospect of bank failures with less concern. Bank and building society deposit insurance in the United Kingdom is of this latter, more limited, kind.

Again, a recent article by Short and O'Driscoll (1983) advocates achieving greater involvement of the private sector in providing competitive deposit insurance by limiting, but *not* abolishing, the role of the FDIC (Federal Deposit Insurance Corporation) and then hoping that a free market would grow up for *additional* private insurance. The authors are themselves worried about the possible adverse effect on confidence of (publicly observable) changes in ratings (p. 21); thus, "Depositors' reaction to a poor insurance rating could involve sudden deposit withdrawals from the affected institution."

Fragile banks would be concerned by such possibilities and by the confidentiality problems arising from having bank examiners probing their business: no private insurance company could possibly provide deposit insurance without having some ability to monitor and to restrict banks' assets and lending activities. The authors ignore the complications that this would involve. For this and other reasons, stronger banks would probably see no reason to apply for such additional insurance. Thus it is dubious whether there would be much demand for (additional) private insurance. Meanwhile, the main risks to the suppliers of deposit insurance do not arise from actuarially calculable events (such as is generally the case, e.g., for personal liabilities, an example mentioned by the authors) but from macro-political-economy developments (e.g., wars, changes in government, and major changes in monetary policy, as happened in the United States in October 1979) that the insurers could neither predict nor themselves influence. Under such circumstances, the natural development of either the demand for, the supply of, or a market in, private deposit insurance is, at best, problematical.

This subject, i.e., the functions, organization, and design of deposit insurance, remains contentious and widely discussed, especially in the United States, where the bad debt problems of commercial banks and S&Ls have caused major problems for the FDIC and the FSLIC, respectively. These difficulties have been analyzed, at much greater length than here, in a couple of important books by Kane (1985) and by Benston, Eisenbeis, Horvitz, Kane, and Kaufman (1986).[5]

Chapter 7
Why Banks Need a Central Bank

1. Banks' Twin Functions in Providing Both Payments and Portfolio Management Services

In chapter 5 it was argued that informational asymmetries between depositor and bank, together with the prospect of contagious bank runs, led to the need for quality control and supervision. One means of achieving that would be to establish a "club" of banks: the Central Bank could be regarded as the independent arbiter and head of that "club." In chapter 6, I dismissed an alternative approach (toward quality control, restitution for depositors suffering from losses, and prevention of runs), in the shape of private insurance programs, as being incapable of providing equivalent support.

Even so, it might be argued that the problem of distinguishing between the services offered by individual banks is, or should be, less severe than the problem of distinguishing between good (and less good) lawyers, accountants, or insurance companies, and yet the Central Bank has a much higher profile than the organizing and supervisory bodies of most other professional and financial services.

Because of such informational asymmetries, many professional services will need some modicum of regulation, whether self-regulation or statutory regulation. Particularly if there is a desirable role for client insurance schemes, the regulator must be able to monitor and to control certain aspects of the activities of the purveyor of the service, e.g., the adequacy of the capital maintained by the business. But the role and functions of a Central Bank in seeking to sustain the health of the banking system generally go well beyond those of regulators of other services, or of regulators acting in other parts of the financial system, such as the SIB (Securities and Investments Board) in the United Kingdom.

It is often argued that such extra attention is due to the twin functions of the banking system in providing both payments and portfolio management services. Thus, Fama[1] describes banks as having two functions, the first being to provide transaction and accounting services and the second being portfolio management. Yet transactions services are carried out by other institutions. e.g., the Post Office and nonbank credit card companies, without much need for special supervision by a Central Bank.[2] More important, I shall argue that it would be perfectly possible and generally safer for transaction services to be provided by an altogether different set of financial intermediaries, i.e., intermediaries providing mutual collective investment in (primarily) marketable securities. If this were to occur, would it make such mutual investment intermediaries, e.g., unit trusts and open-end investment trusts, into banks? Would such intermediaries then become subject to the same risks as banks and need to be subject to the same kind of supervision/regulation?

I believe that there is no necessary reason why banks alone among financial intermediaries should provide transaction services; further, in their role as portfolio managers, banks have much in common with other intermediaries acting in this capacity (though, as I shall argue later, in section 2, certain crucial distinctions remain between the characteristic form of portfolios held by banks as compared with those held by nonbank financial intermediaries). Nevertheless, it is this joint role that is often held to give a special character to banking and to require special treatment for banks through the establishment of a Central Bank, e.g., to provide Lender of Last Resort (LOLR) and other support services for banks in difficulties. Such support goes beyond the assistance envisaged for other financial intermediaries that get into trouble.

Thus, Tobin (1985) states (p. 20) that "the basic dilemma is this: Our monetary and banking institutions have evolved in a way that entangles competition among financial intermediary firms with the provision of transactions media." But what actually are the problems caused by this entanglement? The problem is often seen, and so appears to Tobin, as arising from the propensity of banks, acting as competing financial intermediaries, to run risks of default that, through a process aggravated by contagion, puts the monetary system, whose successful functioning is an essential public good, at risk. Thus, Tobin (1985) states,

> Even if bank managers act with normal perspicuity in the interests of the stockholders, even if all temptations of personal gain are resisted, sheer chance will bring some failures— insolvency because of borrowers' defaults or other capital losses on assets, or inability to meet withdrawals of deposits even though the bank would be solvent if assets' present values could be immediately realised. The probability is multiplied by the essential instability of depositor confidence. News of withdrawals triggers more withdrawals, sauve qui peut, at the same bank, or by contagion at others. For these reasons the banking business has not been left to free market competition but has been significantly regulated.

Tobin's suggestion is, "This problem could be avoided by segregation and earmarking assets corresponding to particular classes of liabilities permitting a depositor in effect to purchase a fund which could not be impaired by difficulties elsewhere in the institution's balance sheet. In this way, a bank would become more like a company offering a variety of mutual funds, just as these companies— which are not insured—are becoming more like banks."

In particular, Tobin, following an earlier suggestion made by Friedman, advocated 100% reserve-backed funds for checkable deposits.[3] Thus, Tobin continues,

> The 100%-reserve deposit proposed ... would be one such (mutual) fund, but there could be others. For example, many households of modest means and little financial sophistication want savings accounts that are safe stores of value in the unit of account. *They can be provided in various maturities without risk by a fund invested in Treasury securities. They can be provided as demand obligations either by letting their redemption value fluctuate with the net asset value* or by crediting a floating interest rate to a fixed value. [Italics added here for emphasis]

With such illustrious and wide support from economists, why has this idea not had more practical success? The concept of a 100% segregated reserve against checkable deposits would, however, reverse the evolution of banking. Initially, goldsmiths received deposits of gold coin from customers and acted purely as safety vaults. It was the realization that it would be profitable, and under most circumstances relatively safe, to loan out some proportion of these reserves to prospective borrowers, in addition to the loans made on the basis of their own capital, that transformed such entrepreneurs into bankers. Naturally, when such early bankers did run into difficulties, by over trading, proposals were made to force such commercial bankers back to stricter segregation. Thus, the forerunner of the Swedish Riksbank, founded by John Palmstruch in 1656, was organized on the basis of two supposedly separate departments: the loan department, financing loans on the basis of longer-term deposits and capital, and the issue department, supplying credit notes on the receipt of gold and specie. But even when Palmstruch's private bank had been taken over by Parliament, "a secret instruction, however, authorized the advance by the exchange department to the lending department of the funds at its disposal, though on reasonably moderate terms."[4]

The reason why such segregation and hypothecation of certain safe assets to checkable deposits will not work in the case of commercial banks is that it largely removes the profitability of banking along with its risks. The regulatory constraint on the banks' preferred portfolio allocation, under such circumstances, would be seen—as historical experience indicates—as burdensome; attempts would be made to avoid or to evade such constraints, e.g., by the provision of substitute transactions media at unconstrained intermediaries that, being free of such constraints, could offer higher returns on such media. Only in the case of non-profit-maximizing banks, such as the Bank of England, divided into two departments on much the same theoretical basis by the 1844 Bank Charter Act, would such segregation be acceptable and not subject to avoidance and evasion. Of course, if the public sector were prepared to subsidize the provision of payment services either by operating them directly itself or "by paying some interest on the 100%-reserves," held in private sector intermediaries, then it could be done; however, in the light of Congress's recent response to suggestions for paying interest on required reserves in the United States, it seems difficult to envisage the public being prepared to vote tax funds for this purpose. Anyhow, there is a simpler and less expensive alternative, which Tobin almost reaches when he comments that the public's savings accounts could be "provided as demand obligations ... by letting their redemption value fluctuate with net asset value."

People are so used to having payment services provided against checkable *fixed nominal value* liabilities, with 100% convertibility of demand deposits, that many have not realized that payment services could be just as easily provided by a mutual collective investment financial intermediary, where the liabilities are units representing a proportional claim on a set of marketable assets. The value of the units fluctuates, of course, with the underlying value of the assets in the portfolio. Because the market value of the portfolio is known, the value of the unit can be published each morning and each depositor then knows how much his or her units are worth. Because there will be a period of float, between writing a check in payment for a purchase and the check being presented for payment at the financial intermediary on which the check is drawn, during which underlying asset values will change, and because the attempt by the mutual funds to meet net outflows by net sales of assets could itself influence prices, one would expect a mutual fund to limit payment services and convertibility. This could be done by requiring some minimum balance in units to be held normally, with a progressive penalty in terms of yield forgone for dropping below this balance, plus some emergency arrangements for occasional overdrafts—say, from an associated bank. The concept of required minimum balance has been adopted often enough by commercial banks, and the public is familiar with it. The checks would, of course, have to be drawn in terms of the numeraire; otherwise, they would not be useful in clearing debts. The value of the drawers' units would change between the date of writing and presenting the check,[5] and therefore, in a period of falling asset prices, there would be a danger of the drawer being overdrawn at the latter date while having had funds to spare at the earlier date; this problem would seem also to be generally soluble by only providing guaranteed payment services up to a minimum credit balance in units, plus an emergency overdraft arrangement, perhaps with an associated bank.

I see no insuperable technical problem to the provision of payment services by mutual collective investment intermediaries in this manner. They would need to hold some liquid reserves, vault cash to pay depositors demanding currency and liquid assets to meet net outflows at times when the fund manager judged that it would be inopportune to realize investments—note that these latter funds are neither for liquidity nor for solvency purposes. Liquidity is always assured by the ability to sell marketable assets, and solvency is assured because the value of liabilities falls with the value of assets. Instead, the desire for liquid assets would arise from a desire to maximize the net asset value of units under varying market conditions, and thus improve reputation, service fees, and managerial earning.[6] Nevertheless, the need to hold at least some vault cash might lower the expected return on the intermediaries' assets; the effect of this on the demand for units should be more than counterbalanced by the improved liquidity to the unit holder of his investments and the associated advantages of being able to use them for transactions purposes.

Be that as it may, the current trend already is for limited transactions services to be provided by investment-managing nonbank financial intermediaries on the basis of depositors' funds, the value of which varies with the market value of the underlying assets. Merrill Lynch cash management service is one example. Certain other unit trusts and mutual funds, such as money market mutual funds, are also providing limited payment services. Similarly, certain building societies and certain mortgage businesses in other countries are already allowing borrowers to draw additional top-up mortgages to a stated maximum proportion of the market value of their houses.[7]

A common response to this idea is that, whereas it would be perfectly possible as a technical matter to provide payment services against liabilities with a varying market value, the public would not happily accept it and it would not succeed in practice. It is argued, for example, that there is a large psychological gulf between being absolutely certain that one has the funds to meet a payment and being 99% certain of that. Is such 100% certainty a general feature of our existing payment system? Unless one monitors one's bank account, outstanding float, etc., continuously and knows exactly what overdraft limits, if any, the bank manager may have set, the willingness of the bank to honor certain check payments will have a probabilistic element.

Lawrence White (1984a, p. 707) put this general case against basing payment services on liabilities with a varying market value most persuasively:

> Demand deposits, being ready debt claims, are potentially superior to mutual fund shares, which are equity claims, in at least one respect. The value of a deposit may be contractually guaranteed to increase over time at a preannounced rate of interest. Its unit-of-account value at a future date is certain so long as the bank continues to honour its obligation to redeem its deposits on demand. No such contractual guarantee may be made with respect to an equity claim. A mutual fund is obligated to pay out after the fact its actual earnings, so that the yield on fund shares cannot be predetermined. In the absence of deposit rate ceiling regulation, the range of anticipated possible returns from holding fund shares need not lie entirely above the deposit interest rate. Risk-diversifying portfolio owners might therefore not divest themselves entirely of demand deposits even given a higher mean yield on mutual funds. It is true that the characteristic pledge of money market mutual funds to maintain a fixed share price, or rather the policy of investing exclusively in short-term highly reputable securities so that the pledge can be kept makes fund shares akin to demand deposits in having near-zero risk of negative nominal yield over any period. The difference between predetermined and post determined yields, between debt and equity, nonetheless remains. The historical fact is that deposit banking did not naturally grow up on an equity basis.

Because the provision of payment services by mutual funds, whose liabilities have a market-varying value, would not only be a somewhat novel concept but would also worry those unused to any probabilistic element in payments, I would expect its introduction to be gradual and probably to start with richer customers better able to cope with such probabilistic concerns. Moreover, such a limited introduction could prevent the mutual funds from making use of economies of scale in the provision of payment services. There are, therefore, some observers who believe that this possible development will fail the practical test of success in the free and open market.

On the other hand, there seems no technical reason why the trend toward the provision of payment services against the value of units in a collective investment fund (up to a minimum balance) should not proceed much further, especially now that technological innovations in the provision of such services, e.g., shared automated teller machines (ATMs), electronic fund transfer (EFT), and home banking, are transforming the production function of payment services, especially in reducing the economies of scale to a network of manned branch buildings. White's arguments (1984a, pp. 707–708) that the provision of payment services by nonbank (mutual fund) intermediaries has been more expensive could be reduced in force, or even reversed, by the new technologies in this field.

Moreover, there would seem considerable cause to welcome such a development, not only for the extra competition that this would inject into this area but also because the characteristics of mutual, collective investment funds should serve to make them naturally more suitable purveyors of payment services than banks. In particular, both the likelihood of a run on an individual bank and of systemic dangers to the monetary system arising from a contagion of fear would be greatly reduced if payment services were provided by mutual collective-investment intermediaries rather than by banks. For example, the announcement of bad news reducing the market value of such an intermediary's assets, assuming an efficient market exists, would immediately reduce the value of depositors' units. There would be no risk of insolvency for the intermediary, and no reason, again assuming an efficient market, for any depositor to withdraw his funds from that intermediary.[8] Again, since the asset portfolios of such intermediaries are publicly reported and their value at any time is exactly ascertainable, there would seem little scope for rumor or fear to take hold. Certainly, if a particular fund manager did significantly worse (better) than average, depositors would find it difficult to distinguish bad (good) luck from bad (good) management and would probably switch funds in sizable amounts to the ex post more successful fund; such switching of money between funds would hardly damage the payment system —rather, the reverse would hold.

There would still be the possibility of a sharp general fall in market values leading depositors to shift en masse out of market valued unit holdings into the fixed nominal value numeraire, thereby forcing the collective investment funds to sell further assets and deepen the asset price depression. Unlike the case of a run on the banks, which raises the subjective probability of failure elsewhere and thus reduces the expected return on holding deposits, at least the falling market values on the assets in the portfolio of the mutual fund should tend to increase the expected running yield on such units and thus act as an offset to the inducement to hold cash. Moreover, it would still be possible for the authorities, perhaps the Central Bank, to undertake open market operations to offset the shift of unit holders into cash, possibly by buying the assets—say, equities—that the funds were selling. There are precedents for such actions: at one time, the Japanese Central Bank intervened to support Stock Exchange values.

Thus, a monetary system in which transaction services were provided to unit holders of collective investment mutual funds would seem inherently safer and more stable than the present system, in which such services are provided to a subset of bank depositors. Indeed, the nature of bank portfolios, largely filled with nonmarketable assets of uncertain true value held on the basis of nominally fixed value liabilities, would seem remarkably unsuited to form the basis of our payment systems. Why did it develop in this way? The answer is, I think, to be found in the accidents of historical evolution. Broad, well-functioning, and efficient asset markets are a reasonably recent phenomenon. Because of people's needs both to borrow and to find a secure home for savings, banks developed well before mutual collective investment funds. The historical form of bank development led them inevitably into the payment business. Thereafter, the economies of scale involved in the existing structure of the payment system, the clearinghouses, branch networks, and the intangibles of public familiarity and the legal and institutional framework left the banks largely—indeed, in some Anglo-Saxon countries absolutely—unrivaled in the provision of payment services.

Owing to the various innovations noted earlier, such bank monopoly of the payment system may now be coming to an end. The authorities should welcome the opportunity to encourage the development of a safer payment system. They should certainly not put obstacles in the way of properly run collective investment funds offering payment services. Indeed, there is a question about what concern the authorities and/or the Central Bank need to feel about the amount of monetary units thereby created and about the state of the intermediaries creating them.[9] So long as such intermediaries abide by their deeds of establishment and restrict their investments to marketable securities of a certain class, with the value of the units adjusted continuously in line, solvency should never be in doubt and would not be affected by the additional offer of payment services. Similarly, liquidity would be assured by marketability. So, it is not clear why a Central Bank should need to impose any additional regulation/supervision over mutual funds offering payment services.

Moreover, in a world where payment services are predominantly provided by monetary units of collective investment funds rather than by banks,[10] why should the authorities pay any particular attention to the quantity of money itself, especially since its nominal value would shift automatically with asset market prices? In such circumstances, how would the quantity of money be measured? Indeed, the intuition of this section is that the monetization of assets is not necessarily limited to a restricted set of financial intermediaries, i.e., banks. A much wider range of financial intermediaries could, in principle, monetize a much wider set of assets than is currently done. In these circumstances, the definition of money would either have to contract to become synonymous with the dominant, "outside" base money, assuming that such money still continues to exist,[11] or become an amorphous concept almost devoid of meaning.

A further proposal, advocated by several American economists,[12] is that banks be forced to revalue their assets at the close of business each day at current market prices ("mark to market"), and that banks be forcibly and immediately closed, taken over by the regulatory authorities, or merged with another bank as soon as their net capital value (solvency) falls close to zero. Since banks would be closed *before* they became insolvent, depositors could receive, and the regulatory/insurance agency could safely provide, 100% insurance cover. There could, of course, still be problems arising from fraud, and the inconvenience of having deposits unusable in a closed bank, even if remaining at guaranteed nominal value, could still lead depositors to seek timely withdrawals from a bank facing difficulties.

If there *were* a known, objective value for all the assets that commercial banks held, so that banks *could* "mark to market" every evening at the market's close, then they would, on current arrangements, be offering fixed nominal value deposit liabilities against market-value-varying assets. This would seem to represent a somewhat risky position for bankers, normally risk-averse individuals, to adopt. I would, therefore, expect that any tendency for banks to restrict, voluntarily or not, their assets to those that had an objective, verifiable market value would be accompanied by a desire to have their liabilities also adjust in line with such changing market values. Thus, proposals to require banks to restrict their asset holdings to such assets as could be given an instantaneous objective market value would, I would expect, lead to a shift toward "mutual fund banking." The familiarity and current preference of depositors for fixed-nominal-value deposits would support the status quo but risk aversion among bankers would provide a driving force for changing to "mutual fund banking."

Note that all three of the proposals outlined here for eliminating the possibility of systemic risk and contagion—i.e., the Tobin/Friedman proposal of requiring that banks only hold "safe" assets against means-of-payments deposits, the Kaufman proposal of "mark-to-market" accounting and rapid closure, and my own of "mutual-fund banking"—all have at their core the requirement that financial intermediaries providing payments services should only hold *marketable* assets. This would seem to indicate that it is the fact that banks' portfolios largely consist of *nonmarketable*, or at least nonmarketed, assets that is largely responsible for the particular problems of ensuring stability within the banking system, a subject to which we turn next in section 2.

2. Bank Portfolios and Central Bank Support

It would appear, therefore, that the provision of payment (monetary) services on units offered by collective investment intermediaries, or perhaps by banks whose assets are restricted to a subset of *marketable* securities, would not, ipso facto, require the involvement of the authorities to monitor and regulate the provision of such services. An associated question is whether the withdrawal of commercial banks from the provision of payment services, so that demand deposits, NOW accounts, and the like were no longer offered, would absolve the Central Bank from its basic concern with the well-being of the banking system. If banks offered only time deposits, CDs, etc., leaving payment and transaction services to others, would there be any need for special support for the banking system?

The answer to this, I believe, is that cessation of payment services would make little difference to banks' riskiness or to the real basis of Central Bank concern with the banking system. There is little or no evidence that demand deposits provide a less stable source of funds than short-dated time deposits, CDs, or borrowing in the interbank market; rather, the reverse appears to be the case.[13] Recent occasions of runs on banks have *not* involved an attempt by the public to move out of bank deposits into cash but have merely produced a flight of depositors from banks seen as excessively dangerous to some alternative placement (not cash). The Fringe Bank crisis in 1973/74 in the United Kingdom and Continental Illinois are instances of this.[14] Earlier, it was suggested that flows of funds from one collective investment fund to another would not have damaging repercussions for the payment system if such funds offered monetized units and provided the bulk of such services. Yet

I shall argue that, even were banking to be entirely divorced from the provision of payment services, such flows between *banks* could be extremely damaging for the economy and would require a continuing support role for a Central Bank to prevent and, if necessary, to recycle such flows.

The reasons why this is so are to be found in the fundamental raison d'être of banking itself. In particular, consider the need for banks to act as intermediaries in the first place. Why cannot people simply purchase the same diversified collection of assets that the bank does? There are, of course, advantages arising from economies of scale and the provision of safekeeping services, but these could be obtained by investing in a collective investment fund. The key difference between a collective investment fund and a bank is that the former invests entirely, or primarily, in marketable assets, while the latter invests quite largely in nonmarketable or, at least, non-marketed assets.

Why do borrowers prefer to obtain loans from banks rather than issue marketable securities? The set-up costs required to allow a proper market to exist have represented, in practice, formidable obstacles to the establishment of markets in the debt and equity obligations of persons and small businesses. Underlying these are the costs of providing sufficient public information to enable an equilibrium fundamental value to be established, e.g., the costs of issuing a credible prospectus, and the size of the expected regular volume of transactions necessary to induce a market maker to establish a market in such an asset. In this sense, the particular role of banks is to specialize in choosing borrowers and monitoring their behavior.[15,16] Public information on the economic condition and prospect of such borrowers is so limited and expensive that the alternative of issuing marketable securities is either nonexistent or unattractive.

Even though banks have such an advantage, vis-à-vis ordinary savers, in choosing and monitoring prospective borrowers, they too will be at a comparative disadvantage, compared with the borrower, in assessing the latter's conditions, intentions, and prospects.[17] Even though there would be advantages in risk sharing resulting from extending loans whose return was conditional on the contingent outcome of the project for which the loans were raised, it would reduce the incentive on the borrower to succeed and the bank would have difficulties in monitoring the ex post outcome. Businessmen, at least in some countries, are sometimes said to have three sets of books, one for the tax inspector, one for their shareholders, and one for themselves. Which one of these would the bank see, or would there be yet another set of books?[18]

In order, therefore, to reduce their own information and monitoring costs while increasing borrowers' incentives to succeed, banks have been led to extend loans on a fixed nominal value basis, irrespective of contingent outcome, with the loan further supported in many cases by collateral and with a duration often less than the intended life of the project to enable periodic reassessment; in addition, a defaulting borrower may face various bankruptcy costs. Even so, both the initial and subsequent valuations of the loan by a bank do depend on information that is generally private between the bank and its borrowers or, perhaps, known only to the borrower.[19]

The true asset value of the bank's (nonmarketed) loans is always subject to uncertainty though their nominal value is fixed, subject to accounting rules about provisions, writeoffs, etc. Under these conditions, it will benefit both bank and depositor to denominate deposit liabilities also in fixed nominal terms. The banks will benefit because the common denomination will reduce the risk that would arise from reduced covariance between the value of its assets and of its liabilities, as would occur, for example, if its liabilities were indexed, say to the RPI (Retail Price Index), and its assets were fixed in nominal value, or alternatively if its assets fluctuated in line with borrowers' profits while its liabilities were fixed in nominal value. The depositor would seek fixed nominal deposits from the bank for the same reason that the bank sought fixed nominal value terms from borrowers: depositors cannot easily monitor the actual condition, intentions, and prospects of their bank, so that information and monitoring costs are lessened and the incentives on the bank to perform satisfactorily are increased by denominating deposits in fixed nominal terms.

John Chant (1987) has similarly identified the nonmarketable nature of bank loans as providing a rationale both for the fixed-nominal-value form of bank deposits and as providing a rationale for external Central Bank regulation. Thus (pp. 27–28, 29, 25, and 51–52, respectively):

> The distinction between marketable and non-marketable securities appears to correspond with the degree to which information required to verify and monitor the value of the investment is publicly supplied by the borrower. While the matter is one of relative emphasis, marketable securities are identified with those for which the borrower supplies the bulk of the information required by investors, whereas with non-marketable securities the lender gathers more of the information.

> The fact that deposit-taking intermediaries are identified with the holding of non-marketable securities suggests that these intermediaries participate in the monitoring and enforcement function to a greater degree than other intermediaries. Moreover, the fixed money value of deposit liabilities appears to be consistent with the need to create appropriate incentives for agents to carry out effective monitoring and enforcement.

> The deposit-taking institution appears to provide a more efficient solution to monitoring and enforcement problems. The agent, who is delegated with the responsibility for monitoring and enforcement, becomes the residual claimant to income. Thus his returns are directly dependent upon his performance. By this interpretation the deposit-taking institution serves as a device to overcome the problems present in any delegation of monitoring and enforcement to agents.

> Deposit-taking institutions have been identified as monitors and enforcers of loan contracts on behalf of the ultimate lenders. This function of managing risk is performed by acquiring non-marketable securities for which the institution takes the responsibility for screening information about the borrower. The value of these assets is specific to the deposit-taking institution who has verified the expected returns from the project, who has gained the information required to

monitor the projects and who understands the problems with respect to enforcement. These dimensions of the customer relationship have to be built up with experience over time. The value of these claims would be less for an outside party who has not gained the knowledge embodied in the customer relationship. In addition to the specific nature of the capital used in intermediation, another aspect of intermediation also appears to favour the use of preventive regulation. Intermediaries typically have many customers, each with rather small amounts on deposit relative to the total. Under these conditions, the transactions costs in co-ordinating recourse for customers appear to be substantial and the incentive for any one depositor to commit resources to increase the probability of a remedy is also slight.

The combination of the nominal convertibility guarantee, together with the uncertainty about the true value of bank assets, also leads, however, to the possibility of runs on individual banks and systemic crises. Since no one actually knows the "true" value of such nonmarketable loans, the fact that the value of a subset of such loans has been found to be impaired at a bank or banks is bound to throw doubt on the position and solvency of other banks believed to have made similar kinds of loan. Moreover, once the nominal convertibility guarantee is established, the effect of better public information on banks' true asset values is uncertain. For example, "hidden reserves" were once justified by practical bankers as likely to reduce the likelihood of runs and to maintain confidence. Again, Central Bankers have been, at most, lukewarm about allowing a market to develop in large syndicated loans to sovereign countries, whose ability to service and repay on schedule was subject to doubt, because the concrete exhibition of the fall in the value of such loans could impair the banks' recorded capital value and potentially cause failures. An economist might ask who was being fooled? Yet, on a number of occasions, financial institutions have been effectively insolvent but, so long as everyone steadfastly averted their gaze, a way through and back to solvency was achieved.

Be that as it may, under these conditions of private and expensive information and fixed nominal value loans, any major flow of funds between banks is liable to have deleterious effects on *borrowers*, as well as on those depositors who lose both wealth and liquidity by having been left too late in the queue to withdraw when the bank(s) suspended payment. Even if the prospects of the borrower of the failed bank are at least as good as on the occasion when the borrower first arranged the loan, the borrower will have to undergo expensive search costs to obtain replacement funds. Assuming the borrower searched beforehand and found the "best" deal, the postsuspension likelihood is that the borrower will obtain less beneficial arrangements.

Bank runs, however, tend to happen when conditions for many borrowers have turned adverse. The suspicion—or, indeed, the knowledge—of that is what prompted the run in the first place. Accordingly, the expected value of the loans of many borrowers will have fallen. If they are forced by the receiver to repay the failing bank to meet the creditors' demands,[20] they would not be able to replace the funds required on the same terms, if at all, from other banks. One of the features of a banking crisis is the tendency for banks to recoil from making further loans to the sector(s) whose difficulties caused the initial solvency problems, whether these be LDCs in the post-1982 period or railroads in some of the nineteenth-century banking panics. At such times of contagious fear, banks often try to upgrade the quality of their assets by shifting from riskier nonmarketable loans to government bonds. At such times, there will be a reassessment of relative riskiness and many classes of borrowers will find credit harder to obtain, not only because certain banks have failed but also because, after such reassessment, borrowers may find continuing banks increasingly unreceptive to their needs. Thus, bank failures will place the economic well-being—indeed, survival—of many borrowers at risk, as well as impairing depositors' wealth.[21] Consequently, flows of funds from suspect banks to supposedly stronger banks can have a severely adverse effect on the economy, even when there is no flight into cash at all. A Central Bank will aim to prevent, or, if that fails, to recycle, such flows, subject to such safeguards as it can achieve to limit moral hazard and to penalize inadequate or improper managerial behavior. As noted in chapter 3, in the absence of a Central Bank, there will be some incentives for commercial banks to act, either independently or collusively, in the same way, i.e., to recycle deposit flows to banks facing liquidity problems and to support or take over potentially insolvent banks. The public good aspect of such actions will, however, be less compelling to competing commercial banks—e.g., why help a competitor that got into trouble through its own fault?—and the risk to their own profit positions of such action more worrying to them than to a Central Bank. Moreover, the usual circumstances of a rescue, at very short notice under conditions of severely limited information, make it more difficult for commercial banks to act conclusively than for an independent Central Bank to act swiftly and decisively.

To summarize and conclude this chapter, it is often claimed that banking is special and particular, requiring additional regulation and supervision by a Central Bank, because banks are unique among financial intermediaries in combining payments' services and portfolio management. I hope to have demonstrated that this is false. Monetary payment services not only could be provided, and are increasingly being provided, by other collective-investment funds but could also be thus provided more safely than by banks. Moreover, the characteristics of such funds are such that their entry into the market for the provision of monetary services need not cause the authorities any extra concern; they could be left to operate under their current regulations. Similarly, if banks were to abandon the provision of payment services and restrict their deposit liabilities to noncheckable form, it would not much reduce bank riskiness. They would still require the assistance of a Central Bank.

All this follows because the really important distinction between banks and other financial intermediaries resides in the characteristics of their asset portfolio, which, in turn, largely determines what kind of liability they can offer: fixed value in the case of banks and market-value related for collective investment funds. It is these latter differences, rather than the special monetary nature of certain bank deposits, that will maintain in future years the distinction between bank and non-bank financial intermediaries.

Chapter 8
Summary and Conclusions

Let me now recapitulate the main arguments of this study.

The costs of acquiring the relevant information (e.g., on bankers' future plans) are too great to allow nonbank individuals to discern accurately which financial institutions are most likely to offer them the best risk/return opportunities. When a failure/default does occur, the same informational deficiencies make it hard to distinguish between causes that are specific to that single institution and common to the group of institutions (i.e., risk of contagion).

The availability of accurate information on other financial institutions is much greater to the institutions themselves. A bank will know much more about its bank competitors than will a member of the public. So the concentration of interbank deposits with conservatively managed, high-reputation, dominating centralized banks is likely to be much greater (and more sensitive to changing news and market assessment) than the distribution of nonbank deposits.

Despite the various advantages in the provision of correspondent services that this concentration can bring, and the growth of clearinghouse associations, so long as the central bank(s) remain *commercial*, mutual banking support and the maintenance of quality control is limited by:

 a. conflict of interest among competitive commercial banks,

 b. conflict between profit maximization and the need to maintain sufficient free reserves to ensure convertibility and the continuation of the monetary regime, and

 c. doubts whether the group of central commercial banks, or the clearinghouse(s), could be sufficiently independent to act as arbiter for the "club" of banks, limiting entry and monitoring behavior, so as to cope with the free rider problem.

The nature of banking risks makes the attempt to use private insurance to protect depositors impracticable. Moreover, the avoidance of moral hazard requires a degree of regulation and interventionist control over the freedom of bankers to choose their preferred portfolios that would seem to require public-sector backing to obtain compliance.

The solution to these problems, which occurred naturally in England (in the face of an uncomprehending, if not antipathetic, legal code in the form of the Bank of England Act of 1844), was the development of the noncompetitive, non-profit-maximizing Central Bank. This model was widely seen as so attractive that it was copied in virtually all other major countries. The process of transition, e.g., from profit-maximizing to non-profit-maximizing, is so hard to achieve that most of these other Central Banks were established by governmental legislation.

The support provided by such Central Bank(s) to the banking system goes well beyond that generally available from central professional bodies to their "club" members. The main rationale that is usually given for this "preferential" treatment is the joint provision by banks of both payment and portfolio management services. I doubt whether this is necessarily so. Instead, I argue that the key feature of banking, which leads to its vulnerability, is its function of providing fixed nominal value loans to borrowers, where information costs make it impossible to observe the actual outcomes of the project, for which the loan was sought, at all accurately. This characteristic induces both the bank and the depositor also to prefer fixed nominal value deposits with a convertibility guarantee, and makes the "true" market value of banks' assets uncertain—indeed, not strictly calculable—which both raises the risk of runs and makes bank supervision, and support, more necessary and more difficult.

Appendix: Central Banks in Europe and Japan at the End of the Nineteenth Century

Introduction

The development of Central Banks, from concentrating on note issue and the finance of government to an acceptance of responsibility for regulating the banking system, at both the macro and micro levels, was reviewed in the main text. The importance of the Central Bank acting in a noncompetitive, non-profit-maximizing manner was noted. Much of that analysis was colored by the historical experience of England, and also of the United States, for which Timberlake (1978) is informative. This appendix, by contrast, seeks to examine the record of several European countries and Japan.

It is possible to do so at a common date by recourse to the voluminous studies of the National Monetary Commission. Following the financial crisis of 1907, which centered in New York, Congress appointed the National Monetary Commission to consider, inter alia, the need for, and functions of, Central Banks. It collected papers, some specially commissioned, about the history of several Central Banks, mostly European, which filled volumes;[1] additionally, it held interviews on these issues with bankers from savings banks, commercial banks, and Central Banks in a number of countries.[2] These studies provide an easily accessible, and extremely valuable, comparative snapshot of Central Banking as it had developed in a variety of (primarily European) countries.

The Reichsbank

The most extensive documentary coverage by the National Monetary Commission (NMC) of any foreign country was of the development of Central Banking in Germany. Volume X reprinted a work published under the auspices of the Reichsbank in 1900, on the occasion of its 25th anniversary, to describe its establishment, organization, and operations, plus a series of articles, a report of the proceedings of a bankers' convention (Hamburg 1907), the revised Bank Act of June 1909, etc. There were four additional volumes of papers concerning the German banking system in the NMC series: Vols. XI, XII, XIII, and XIV (as already noted in note 1 of the Introduction to this appendix). In the *Interviews*, the longest were for England (120 pages), France (146 pages), and Germany (166 pages). It is, therefore, fitting to begin with Germany.

The pamphlet entitled *The Reichsbank*, published under the auspices of the Reichsbank itself, makes it clear from the outset that the primary purpose of the foundation of the Central Bank was to unify and to organize the note issue. The opening sentences of the pamphlet are as follows:

> The newly established German Empire found in the organization of the coinage, paper money, and bank-note systems, an urgent and difficult task. Probably in no department of the entire national economic system were the disadvantages of the political disunion of Germany so clearly defined as in this; in no economic department were greater advantages to be expected from a political union.
>
> Although the customs union (Zollverein) had happily united the greater part of Germany in a commercial union, similar attempts in monetary affairs had met with but modest success, and were absolutely fruitless in banking.
>
> The inconvenience most complained of was the multiplicity and variety of the different coinage systems (seven in all) in the different states, also the want of an adequate, regulated circulation of gold coins.

A second main purpose, and function, of the Reichsbank was to improve and to organize the system of countrywide payment. Before its establishment there had been no clearinghouses in Germany. Then, in 1883, one was started in Berlin under the auspices of the Reichsbank, and with settlement occurring through transfers of bal ances held at the Reichsbank. The Reichsbank established branches in all main centers, not only for note issuing purposes, but also to facilitate longer distance payments within Germany. In effect, the Reichsbank operated and managed the payments system. The successful development of the transfer system encouraged a rapid growth in the use of check payments (and the growing use of bank deposits) during the years 1875–1910.[1]

Apart from a short, administrative section on the Reichsbank's role in receiving and making payments for the German imperial government (chapter VIII of *The Reichsbank*), there was little discussion in the Reichsbank's own account of its functions and operations (i.e., *The Reichsbank*) of the services that a Central Bank could provide to a government, especially in times of war. That subject, however, was still at the back of many peoples' minds.[2] Moreover, the Reichsbank had been founded along the model of, and indeed quite largely by taking over, the Prussian State Bank, and this had been founded and functioned primarily as a state bank to further the financial interests of Prussia.[3] Despite this parentage, the links between the Reichsbank and the imperial government did not play a major role in the early years of its existence; no doubt the absence of war and the dramatic growth of the German economy reduced the imperial government's need for financial support.

The management and direction of the Reichsbank involved a mixture (combination) of public and private appointees. Although the government could always, when it really needed, call the tune through the officially appointed directorate, there were private shareholders, who elected a central committee (Zentralausschuss) that met monthly with the president of the Reichsbank directorate, (*The Reichsbank*, chapter I). Contemporary comment, as evidenced by the various articles in *Renewal of Reichsbank Charter*, suggest that the influence of the private sector representatives on the Reichsbank was felt to be considerable, and that there were felt to be many advantages in maintaining a mixed, rather than a purely state-run, Central Bank.[4]

The share of the shareholders in the profits of the Reichsbank was, however, limited by law. At the time of the National Monetary Commission, "Shareholders received $3\frac{1}{2}$ per cent dividends and one-fourth of the excess, the Imperial Government receiving the other three-fourths." [5] Although the shareholders had some limited share in the Reichsbank's profits, it was made absolutely clear that the Reichsbank did not seek to maximize profits. Profitability was a very secondary consideration. Thus in the *Interviews*, Dr. von Glasenapp, director of the Reichsbank, replied, when asked about the regard paid to the profits of stockholders, that "our stock holders have secondary consideration," and subsequently affirmed (p. 353) that "the Reichsbank must be considered in the first place as a public institution which has to take care of the public interest, and that it is secondarily a money-making institution."

Although the Reichsbank did not regard itself as a profit-maximizing institution, concern with its profits did on occasion play some slight role. Thus in *The Reichsbank* (p. 230) it was noted that in the period 1876–1879, ".... Officials of the Reichsbank were placed in a serious dilemma: the decrease of profit-yielding funds ... urged a reduction of discount and lombard rates. On the other hand [there was a need to build up gold reserves]." Also private commercial banks often underbid the Reichsbank discount rate; rather than sell bills to make their rate effective, the Reichsbank sought to place (no doubt to no avail) legal restrictions on private banks to underbid them (see *The Reichsbank*, pp. 347–348).

What, then, did determine the course of the Reichsbank's day-to-day monetary operations (note-issuing and payments' transfer functions aside), if profit-maximizing did not?[6] *The Reichsbank* (p. 202) stated that "the most important and likewise the most difficult task of the Bank is to bring about the greatest possible equalization of fluctuations in money demands and to be at all times in a position to redeem its notes and to meet its other demand liabilities," which I would interpret as maximum stabilization and accommodation of the financial system, subject to the constraints of the Gold Standard. Professor W. Lexis. "Concerning the Renewal of the Reichsbank Charter," stated[7] that "the nature of its [Reichsbank's] task is that it shall maintain the value of the monetary unit as stable as possible...."

For a statement of the advantages of discretionary management, within the constraints of seeking both to maintain the Gold Standard and also to foster the well-being of the financial system and business more broadly, see the paper by Dr. Stroell,[8] "Concerning the Renewal of the Privilege of the Reichsbank, and of the Private Note Banks," especially his statement (p. 249) that "it [the Reichsbank] must establish the interest rate after careful consideration of all pertinent conditions...."

The relations of the commercial banks with the Reichsbank were aided by the fact that the nature of business undertaken by the latter was restricted, by legislation and by subsequent operation, to limit the extent of competition between them. The Reichsbank could only offer interest-bearing deposits up to the amount of its capital and reserves, by statute, but after a short interval it ceased to maintain any such interest-bearing deposits (see *The Reichsbank*, pp. 120–121), whereas Herr Mankiewitz of the Deutsche Bank (*Interviews*, p. 386) responded to the question "Is it customary for you and other banks to pay interest on deposits?" with "Yes, we always pay interest." Moreover, even the non-interest-bearing deposits of the Reichsbank were offered without (*The Reichsbank*, p. 122) "further services of any kind from the Bank," so naturally such business from ordinary retail customers was minimal. Nevertheless, the services that the Reichsbank provided in facilitating transfers, and managing the clearinghouses, were such as to provide it with growing, voluntarily held non-interest-bearing balances; in 1908 52% of its balances (by value) came from bankers, and 48% from various industrial and commercial companies (see *Renewal of Reichsbank Charter*, p. 60).

Moreover, the assets that the Reichsbank could hold were largely restricted to high-grade bills, so it did not compete with the large commercial banks over most of their business. With there, thus, being little, or no, competition between the Reichsbank and the Banks,[9] the latter were generally, at least in public, almost fulsomely effusive in their praise of the Reichsbank.

Besides the transfer, note issuing, and other services that the Reichsbank provided, the commercial banks came to rely on it for additional liquidity. They saw their reserve strength, *not* as lying so much in their existing cash reserves, but as resting on their ability to sell, and thus liquefy, commercial paper at the Reichsbank. Thus

Herr Mankiewitz, of the Deutsche Bank, stated (*Interviews*, p. 372) that "the great strength of our financial system in Germany is the Reichsbank. Under that system the question of our own cash reserve is of secondary importance, as we can at all times convert our holdings of commercial paper into cash at the Reichsbank." Similarly, Herr Schuster and Herr Nathan of the Dresdner Bank (*Interviews*, p. 395), when asked if they sought to maintain a normal cash ratio, said, "No, we are practically indifferent to the percentage, as long as we know that we have on hand a sufficient amount of prime bills."

It is clear, therefore, that the Reichsbank had early on assumed the full Central Banking macro function of regulating the financial system, and that its position as a noncompetitive, non-profit-maximizing institution aided it in this role. It successfully passed a testing period in 1901. Herr Schuster and Herr Nathan of the Dresdner Bank (*Interviews*, p. 398) reported, "We had a very serious crisis here in 1901. It was a money crisis, and at that time the Reichsbank was very liberal in extending credits. The Reichsbank feels that it has a patriotic duty to preserve the credit of the Empire. It is a state institution." Thus, in general and in its macro function, "The Reichsbank has always been the last resort and a thoroughly reliable resort." [10]

Although the Reichsbank, therefore, played the role of lender of last resort to the system as a whole, by purchasing prime bills on the open market and expanding its "excess" note issue, at times of financial stress, it appeared to be able to avoid direct contact with individual banks, notably as a lender of last resort in specific cases. Moreover, there were a number of bankruptcies during these years, of which the Leipziger Bank was the most important,[11] from which the Reichsbank appeared able to stand aside. Furthermore, the Reichsbank seemed to play no part in the regulation or examination of commercial banks, such as it was,[12] or even to play much of a public role in trying to require them to publish more information on their operations and balance sheets; there is no mention in *The Reichsbank* of *any* such direct relationships with commercial banks.

Some economists, and other commentators, have commended the separation of the macro function, of managing the development of the financial system as a whole, from the micro function involving the supervision, regulation, and acting as lender of last resort to individual banks: they commend it usually on the grounds that concern with the micro function distorts the conduct of the macro function, so that, if the two functions can be separate, they should be.

I would argue, however, that the nature of banking business is such that the two functions are, *generally*, not separable. The reasons why they could be (successfully) separated in Germany during these years include the following. First, the public mostly used cash as a means of payment, and deposits more as a savings medium (there was relatively little use of checks as a medium of exchange); the ratio of cash to sight deposits was, therefore, high.[13]

Furthermore, the ratio of capital to deposits was much higher in German (than in English) banks.[14] The German banks were much nearer to portfolio managers of savings than to pure deposit banks: indeed, there was in Germany at this time some academic discussion, led by Prof. Adolph Wagner, whether the two forms of banking should not be rigorously separate, and differently regulated.[15] Be that as it may, the structure of the German banking system made it less subject to the effects of contagious panic. Without the danger of contagion, the Central Bank can deal only with the system as a whole, leaving supervision of the individual unit to other bodies. Once contagion, however, becomes a real concern—as it generally does in modern banking—that separation can no longer be made.

The Swiss National Bank

The Swiss National Bank, founded by the law of October 1905, closely followed the model of the Reichsbank, with mixed public and private ownership, and limitations on the dividends payable to the private shareholders. The form of ownership and control had been a matter of considerable debate for some time:[1] a legislative article to establish a Central Bank with the exclusive right to note issue had been adopted in 1891, "but remained a dead letter, as the Legislature was unable to decide whether they would have a state bank or an absolutely private bank."[2]

Indeed, it took "twenty years fighting" in Parliament between the radicals, wanting a purely state bank, and the conservatives, who wanted a federal bank, to reach the eventual compromise.[3] The reasons for its establishment were much the same as in the case of the Reichsbank. Note issue had previously been undertaken by the individual cantonal banks, some 36 in 1881.[4] Earlier in the nineteenth century, "it was very difficult to popularize these bank notes, the security of which was doubted, not without some reason. Outside their home Canton they would either not be given in payment at all or only at a certain discount."[5]

The first step toward improving the position was the adoption of a concordat in 1862 among the stronger banks, "to accept one another's notes in payment, and started a kind of clearing and circulating system among themselves."[6] In practice, however, the Swiss banks collectively relied on the Banque de France to provide Central Banking facilities, and when those facilities became unavailable, owing to the Franco-Prussian war, they each tried "to fortify their position" and a major crisis developed.[7]

This convinced experts and informed opinion that something needed to be done, but there was disagreement whether it would be sufficient to legislate for tighter regulations on the existing rights of cantonal banks to issue notes or to establish a federal bank with a monopoly over the note issue.[8] After the defeat, by referendum, of an earlier law to control the independent note issue in 1875, a law to control and constrain the note issues of the cantonal banks was passed in 1881.[9]

Even the critics of this law accepted that it "put a stop to the wildest excesses of the days of cantonal sovereignty,"[10] and thereafter there was "no distrust of bank notes,"[11] partly because of "very rigid supervision by a federal comptroller"[12] and a law requiring 40% backing in legal tender (and the remaining 60% in specified liquid assets).[13] Despite this reform of the note-issuing regulations in 1881, the agitation for the establishment of a Central Bank with monopoly control of the note issue continued. There were several reasons for this. Although the safety of the note issue was protected, the form of the law of 1881, which included a tax on the *authorized* amount of notes, not the amount in *circulation*, encouraged the banks to try to keep the maximum possible outstanding at all times.[14] This put downward pressure on interest rates, (despite the attempts of the banks to establish a minimum discount rate by agreement in 1894 and again in 1898)[15] and led to an outflow of specie during normal times, while preventing any elasticity in currency at times of pressure.[16] A further crisis ensued in 1886, when rumors of war circulated, and the banks, again fearing that they could not turn to the Banque de France, restricted credit severely.[17] This second experience confirmed the belief of many observers that independent note-issuing banks could not respond appropriately in a crisis. Moreover, there was a desire for Switzerland to join the Gold Standard, but the "... necessary preparations could not be commenced until the decentralized bank-note system had been got rid of, and in its place had been established a strong central bank which also offered, by its discount and exchange policies, sufficient guaranties that the reform would be successfully carried through."[18]

Meanwhile, in the absence of such a Central Bank, not only was the internal discount rate considered to be subject to excessive competitive underbidding,[19] but also the Swiss banks' reaction to exchange rate pressure was such as to allow undesirable speculation and arbitrage.[20]

Furthermore, whereas the law of 1881 generally required adequate asset backing[21] against note issue, there were no constraints on the asset backing against deposits, even sight deposits; so without the support of a Central Bank, the weaknesses of some Swiss banks "were not only a menace to particular weak banks, but they actually endangered the entire system of the Swiss banks of issue."[22]

For such reasons, the campaign to establish a Central Bank in Switzerland continued. Despite certain setbacks, such as the defeat in the 1896 referendum[23] and the long-drawn-out battle over the form of ownership and site of the Bank, it was finally established by a referendum in October 1905. Besides its note issuing function, "the National Bank has for its principal objects to regulate the money market of the country, and to facilitate payments and transfers of money": the latter, transfer and payment facilities, had been unsatisfactory beforehand.[24] The SNB (Swiss National Bank) was not allowed by statute to allow interest on deposits to anyone but the Confederation. This was precisely designed "... to prevent the National Bank from competing with other banks."[25] Moreover, "The principal purpose of the Bank is to regulate the Swiss monetary system, not to make dividends and to issue notes."[26]

So, following the example of the Reichsbank, the SNB was established at the outset as a non-profit-maximizing, noncompetitive Central Bank, for the purpose of undertaking the macro function of regulating the monetary system, while the micro function of individual bank supervision was already in the hands of a federal comptroller and the inspectors of banks.

The Banque de France

The Banque de France was founded in 1800 by Napoleon. Although the circumstances of the time made it "... impossible to obtain ... trustworthy details or exact information concerning the circumstances which led to the creation of the Bank.... All the facts so far known tend to prove that First Consul Bonaparte took the initial steps toward founding the Bank of France. He could not get what he wanted from the free banks. On the other hand, he felt that the Treasury needed money, and wanted to have under his hand an establishment which he could compel to meet his wishes."[1] Previously, in 1797, the Paris private bankers had founded a private financial institution, the Caisse des Comptes Courants,[2] to provide quasi-Central Banking functions for themselves, including note issue: under strong official prompting the Caisse was merged with the new Banque de France.[3] Besides the Caisse des Comptes Courants, there were other note issuing banks in Paris at that time, notably the Caisse d'Escompte du Commerce; after strenuous official pressure was applied, these were all closed, or forced to merge with the Banque de France, and by 1803 the Bank of France had the exclusive privilege of issuing bank notes in Paris.[4]

Although the Bank of France was thus founded through official prompting, and with official support, it was not owned by the state; it was founded by, and retained, private shareholders (though its earliest subscribers included the Bonapartes and their supporters).[5]

Although the Bank was naturally aware of the importance of its relationship with the government, its management and direction in the first couple of years remained in private hands, i.e., in the committee of three chosen from the regents named by the stockholders. Unfortunately the managers did not succeed in preventing the crisis of 1805 (caused by rumors that Napoleon had removed the gold reserve from the Bank in order to finance his campaign). Napoleon was alarmed, and thought that "... crisis was caused by the bankers themselves. He was not overfond of them, especially since the Consulate, when they had refused him money, and he distrusted them because he saw that they made use of the Bank to advance their own interests."[6]

Accordingly, by law in 1806, he replaced the private management by a governor and two deputy governors, appointed directly by the head of state and advised by the minister of finance.[7] Thus Napoleon "... transformed the Bank of France in reality into a state bank whose capital was furnished by private individuals."[8]

Although control thus effectively passed into the hands of public servants, the profits of the Bank remained largely with the shareholders. Initially, they received a dividend of 6% of the original capital, plus two-thirds of the remaining profits.[9] At every occasion on which the privileges of the Bank subsequently came up for legislative review during the nineteenth century, the government of the day took its opportunity to take for itself another slice of the profits of seignorage.[10] For example, it was widely noted that the profitability of the Bank rose when interest rates were high[11] (indeed, it was remarked that the rising price of Bank shares on the Bourse acted as a counterweight to falling asset values elsewhere when interest rates rose): so when the Bank's charter was renewed in 1897, the proceeds resulting from an increase in the discount rate above 5% was to revert to the state, not to the shareholders.[12]

This mixed form of organization, with the direction entrusted to public servants but owned by private shareholders, as established by Napoleon in 1806, proved to be enduring. Through the, often violent, political changes during the nineteenth century (notably in 1848), the Bank generally managed to retain the close confidence of the government of the day (whatever its political color), while the shareholders were kept happy by regular dividends and a high share price. Indeed, after the defeat of France in the Franco-Prussian war of 1870, another advantage was claimed for retaining private ownership: thus Liesse[13] writes, "The foreign enemy, it is true, could not, because of the private character of the Bank, consider its wealth as spoils of war, without trampling under foot international law. The case would have been entirely different had the Bank been a State bank. This is an advantage not to be neglected...." A more civilized century! Meanwhile, the direction of the Bank by officials appointed by the head of state implied that the Bank would seek to pursue the public interest rather than private profit maximization.[14]

Although the organizational and managerial structure of the Bank, established in 1806, enabled it to steer successfully through the political troubles in France in the nineteenth century, its record in sustaining the French financial system during the first half of the nineteenth century was checkered—indeed, in many respects unsatisfactory. At the micro level, it spent more effort in competing with other, potentially rival, banks than in fostering the development of French banking. In particular, the Bank had been granted the exclusive privilege of note issue in Paris, but the situation in other centers and the country more widely was left unclear, except that banks, which at that time would expect generally to be note issuing, could not "... be organized in the provinces without the consent of the Government:"[15]

The decree of 1808 "specified that the Bank should create in the principal provincial towns branch offices, chiefly in places where they would serve the needs of commerce.... The Bank had the exclusive right of issue only in the towns where it had branch offices. The State could therefore give this privilege to other establishments in other places."[16] Compared with the energy shown by the Reichsbank in opening branches after 1875, the Banque de France showed remarkably little enthusiasm for establishing a branch network; indeed, it was continually having to be prodded throughout the nineteenth century to extend the number of its branches.[17] Two motives for the Bank's reluctance to extend its branch system were advanced by Patron:[18] the first was that such branches were often not profitable (if this explanation is indeed correct, it is an example of the baleful effect that concern with profitability can have on Central Banking functions); the second reason was that the business of such branches in discounting, arranging payments, and transfers would conflict and compete with the business of the small, local, privately run banks.

Whatever the reason, and neither of the motives suggested above seems fully compelling, the Bank did not move rapidly to extend its note-issuing privilege nationwide by establishing branches. Nevertheless, it used its influence, whenever possible, to prevent competitors from filling the gap, and its response to other banking institutions was generally one of hostility.[19] Even when the financial institution was not so clearly a direct note-issuing competitor, as in the case of Jacques Lafitte's Caisse Générale du Commerce et de l'Industrie, founded 1837, the Bank did not extend any help when it ran into difficulties in 1847.[20] Indeed, when the Crédit Mobilier had such an initial success (founded 1852, apogee of success 1855, failed 1867), the Banque de France temporarily (1858–1861) moved away from its previous policy of limiting its assets to three-name commercial paper toward operating in securities. Liesse asks rhetorically,[21] "... was it the example of the company [Credit Mobilier] which induced the Bank of France at that time to follow the same course? It is rather difficult to say."

Despite the hostility of the Bank, several departmental banks of issue had been established in the 1830s. They were not, however, able to weather the panic of 1848. They asked for their notes to be made legal tender (cours force). Since their notes had been subject to restrictions (only serving as local currency), the authorities did not feel that their notes could be made legal tender while the departmental banks retained their existing form. So these banks were forcibly merged with the Bank of France, and led somewhat accidentally to "... the monopoly of the Bank of France as a bank of issue. The latter owed this advantage to the ability of its administrators, to the lack of cooperation among the departmental banks, and, finally to the tendency of the French to centralize everything."[22]

Although the Bank finally achieved a complete note-issuing monopoly in 1848, only briefly and unsuccessfully challenged by the

Pereire brothers with the Bank of Savoy in the early 1860s, the French banking system was in a sorely underdeveloped state at mid-century. Apart from the old-established and strong private banks in Paris, e.g., the houses of Rothschild, Davillier, d'Eichtal, Mallet, Hottinguer, and Henrotte and Muller (which generally appeared to have had a happy relationship with the Banque de France), the banking system outside Paris was weak and fragmented, largely consisting of small, private, family concerns, local banks of unknown number and size, which did not offer checking accounts, but took in limited amounts of time and savings deposits, made loans on the basis of personal knowledge, and executed transfers, at a price. The Banque de France did undertake transfers and helped to facilitate payments, but its branches were, as already noted, few, its customers generally limited to banks, large commercial institutions, etc., and its transfers bore charges.[23] No clearinghouse was founded until 1872, in Paris, and none elsewhere before 1910: even then many more transfers went through the Bank of France than through the clearinghouse.[24] It is invidious to assign blame for this limited development, though part of the blame should be attributed to an unsatisfactory legal infrastructure. Thus there was no proper law to regulate the use of checks before 1865.[25] The requirement that joint stock banks could only be chartered by the Council of State, prior to the reform of the law on joint stock organizations, e.g., in 1867, lent itself to inertia and obstruction.[26] Nevertheless, in the first half of the nineteenth century the Banque de France was hardly carrying out appropriate Central Bank micro functions.

From the outset, the macro function that the Bank's founder imposed on it was to stabilize the discount rate. Thus Patron reports,[27] "Napoleon said: 'I have created the Bank in order to allow discount at 4 per cent'. This was a very low rate one hundred years ago, and these few words show that the founder of the Bank meant, also, that it should remain stable."[28] Earlier, by the decree of 1808, the rate of discount in the branches was legally "... fixed at 5 per cent. Once a year the Minister of Finance was to make a report on the transactions of each branch office, and propose, if it were judged necessary, a lowering of the rate."[29] This desire for stability in interest rates remained a continuing theme in France; Patron quotes

Courcelle Seneuil as claiming that "while it is not possible to reach absolutely fixed and uniform rates of discount and credit conditions, the nearer they are approached the nearer we are to perfection."[30] Moreover, prior to 1857, the usury laws had restricted the Bank from raising its discount rate above 6%.

Even within its limited area of freedom, the Bank had sought to hold rates steady; indeed, the discount rate remained fixed for some thirty years up till 1848.[31] In order to achieve this stability in quoted rates, the Bank had to adopt certain stratagems. In the 1818 crisis, the Bank maintained a constant published discount rate but reduced the tenor of bills that it would discount from three months to 45 days:[32] in the crisis brought on by the Crimean War, 1855, it repeated this maneuver, though the tenor was only limited to seventy-five days.[33] In 1846, the Bank made special arrangements to acquire specie and borrowed from Russia.[34] It bought gold, at a premium, in 1847, 1855–1857, and 1864.[35] Up until 1897, the retention of bimetallism allowed the Bank to redeem its notes in whichever metal was less valuable, though it is not clear how much use the Bank made of this option.[36] In 1870, the Bank was authorized, in order to conserve its metallic reserve, to issue small notes.[37] Finally, when all else failed, in 1848 and 1870, the Bank applied for, and obtained, legal tender (cours force) and suspended convertibility, though in each case returning to convertibility shortly after the crisis was over.[38]

So from the beginning, the Bank of France was entrusted with a rather more specific macro function (than other nascent Central Banks)—to keep the discount rate in the main financial market (i.e., Paris) as stable as possible, consistent with a general desire to remain on a metallic standard and to amass sufficient metallic reserves. Considering the difficulties of this remit, it succeeded rather well in achieving such stability, though in the occasional crises that occurred from 1805 to 1870, it had to resort to various stratagems, and in extremis to the suspension of convertibility in 1848 and 1870.

The Bank's competition with, and hostility to, other banking institutions that had so marred the first half of the century diminished thereafter. There is, however, still a hint in Liesse's historical account that the Bank had had a hand in restricting the functions of the newly established (in 1848) Comptoir d'Escompte to being a bank of discount (necessarily established, with strong government support, because the crises of 1847 and 1848 had seen the collapse of so many existing banks that there were not enough left to discount commercial paper and to provide a third name to make the paper acceptable to the Banque de France), by limiting its ability to accept current accounts to $1\frac{1}{2}$ times capital.[39] Thereafter, the Bank had to fight off the challenge to its note-issuing monopoly by the Pereire brothers and the Bank of Savoy, which led to the Enquiry of 1865 that figures so largely in Vera Smith's *The Rationale of Central Banking*.

Bagehot gave evidence at that enquiry. Whether or not that enquiry influenced thinking at the Banque de France, their actions at the micro level were subsequently much more supportive to the French banking system in the final third of the century. Following the English example of deposit banking (with no note issue), the large credit societies—the Crédit Industriel and Commercial, the Société Générale, and the Crédit Lyonnais, established in the late '50s and early '60s[40]—formed with the Comptoir d'Escompte the big four commercial banks.[41] In their normal day-to-day business activities, the operations of the Banque de France and of these four big commercial banks appeared, to themselves, to be more complementary than competitive. The Bank did not offer interest-bearing deposits to the general public, while the commercial banks did; the Bank primarily rediscounted three-name commercial paper, while the commercial banks extended loans and advances. We have earlier noted the accusation that the Banque de France never aimed to attract a wider public clientele, limiting its customers to other banks and large businesses.[42] Indeed, Liesse claims[43] that the "... parallel development of branch offices and agencies of the Bank of France, and of the agencies of the credit companies, greatly aided the development of the latter"[44] (by allowing the credit companies to rediscount when in need). Certainly, the main commercial banks denied any competition between themselves and the Bank.[45] Moreover, the Banque de France, at times of crisis, also took more direct steps to support the commercial banks.

The first example of direct intervention, lender of last resort action, by the Banque de France (to quell instability in the financial system) did not, however, involve lending to a bank, but to the Stock Exchange. Liesse records[46] that "when the storm burst in January [1882], the stockbrokers of Paris and Lyons, who had not paid sufficient attention to the consequences of this frantic speculation, could not meet their engagements. The Bank of France intervened at this moment and advanced 80,000,000 to that parquet of the Paris Bourse and 100,000,000 to that of Lyons—all this being secured by bills by exchange and collateral." Almost immediately thereafter, in February 1882, the Bank of France intervened again to support several banks following the crash of the Union Générale. Patron comments[47] that "from this period dates the prosperity of the better managed banks, which, having remained unharmed, gathered in the customers of the discredited institutions." Then, in 1889, the Bank felt compelled—partly, Liesse suggests, to prevent disruption occurring on the eve of the opening of the 1889 Exposition—to provide support to the Comptoir d'Escompte, following its disastrous speculation in copper and the suicide of its president. Despite the support, the Comptoir had to be liquidated and reorganized, under the guidance of a former governor of the Bank of France.[48] Shortly afterward, in March 1891, the Bank intervened again, to support the Société des Dépôts et Comptes Courants.[49]

Thus, before the Bank of England demonstrated in the Baring crisis that it had taken on the micro function of arranging lender of last resort support to financial institutions in difficulties, the Banque de France had led the way. The "moral hazard" problem was soon recognized; thus Liesse comments,[50] "it has been asked if the help supplied so quickly by the Bank of France to insolvent credit companies was not of a nature to diminish the prudence of the administrators of these companies, and to give the public the assurance that a tutelary establishment would always come forward to protect the funds deposited in these establishments." So, the way lay open for the Banque de France to extend its micro function into regulation[51] and supervision, the more so since there was virtually no governmental supervision of banks.[52]

After the disastrous defeat of the Franco-Prussian War, the natural strength of the French economy soon reasserted itself. The war indemnity to Germany was successfully financed and paid,[53] the Bank of France resumed convertibility, and the current account became persistently strong and positive; despite large capital outflows, this allowed the Bank to amass a large gold reserve.[54] So strong was the position of the Bank that, from 1897 until 1914, it was able to maintain its traditional preference[55] for stable interest rates without resort to the strategems earlier mentioned. Indeed, it began to use its gold reserves in a strategic international fashion, making loans, e.g., to the Bank of England in May 1906, and shipping gold to foreign centers in order to relieve and prevent financial crises abroad, before they might disturb financial conditions domestically in France.[56]

So, besides having successfully developed the micro functions of Central Banking, the Banque de France was also able to satisfy the French penchant for stable interest rates in conducting the macro function of monetary management during the years before 1914.

The Swedish Riksbank

The best known fact about the Riksbank is that it was founded in 1668, 26 years before the Bank of England, and thus is the oldest established Central Bank. While this is strictly the case, in another sense it can be said to be misleading.

First, the bank was actually initially founded as a private institution in 1656 under charter granted to John Palmstruch. This ran into difficulties in 1664;[1] the government, perhaps because of loans made to some of its members, wished to support its continued existence, and, after a period in which the government continued the bank's operations as a supposedly temporary expedient, it was reorganized under the authority and supervision of Parliament in 1668.[2] It was not, however, called the Riksbank (or National Bank) until 1867, but the Rikets Standers Bank, the Bank of the Estates of the Realm. It was not in any sense under the control of the executive, the Crown; indeed its independence from the Crown was jealously guarded. Even in 1897, from which date the Riksbank may, perhaps, be said to have become a Central Bank, "The jealousy of interference on the part of the Crown finds an expression in a section of the 1897 act relating to occasions when a representative of the executive government may be sent to confer with the managing committee of the bank. The committee is forbidden to decide the question in hand so long as the Crown's agent is present with them. They are thus assured opportunity for private discussion and independent action." [3]

Instead, the bank operated effectively as a commercial bank, with two peculiar features. First, for almost all the period from its foundation in 1656 until the 1830s, it was the *only* bank in Sweden,[4] as well as the primary source of notes.[5,6] Second, as already noted, it came to be owned and supervised by Parliament in 1668. Despite such parliamentary oversight, the bank ran into difficulties in 1726, of the typical kind relating to overissue of notes in connection with unsecured loans to the government; the government then came to its aid by declaring its notes legal tender, which they remained until 1873, when Sweden joined the Gold Standard, and the medium of redemption changed from notes of the Riksbank to gold—this is, I believe, the longest consecutive period during which a bank's notes have been legal tender. In 1745, as a result of further overissue, the bank was allowed to cease redemption in metal (by then silver), and its notes depreciated and were not fixed again, at a new lower rate, in terms of silver until 1776 (despite an order by Parliament in 1760 to reduce loans, in order to lower the amount and raise the value of the note issue—an order that apparently had no effect)—see Flux (1911, p. 20). In 1810, in the face of the financial pressures of war, the bank again suspended silver payments, and convertibility was not restored until 1834 (Flux, 1911, p. 28). So, in the early period of its history, various pressures prevented the bank from maintaining convertibility into specie for long stretches of time.

Not only did the bank fail to maintain convertibility, but also it had "... long been felt that the banking requirements of the country could not be satisfactorily met by a single central institution," that facilities should be provided in centres other than Stockholm, and "... that the needs of industry and commerce could be met better by the creation of private [banking] enterprises" (Flux, 1911,

p. 30). Accordingly, a decree of 1824 authorized the establishment of private banks, and it was specificly laid down that these private banks should have no aid from, or involvement with, the state, even at times of difficulty. The main purpose of the banks was to support industry, commerce, etc., by making loans and facilitating payments. No mention was made of note issue in the original decree, but the charters of the original banks all provided for note issue (Flux, 1911, p. 33). The subject of note issue was subsequently covered by a revised enactment in 1846, which limited the note issue of each bank to an amount equal to its cash (specie, Riksbank notes, and balances) plus securities up to an amount equal to half its capital (Flux, 1911, pp. 33–36).

These private, note-issuing banks, the enskilda banks, were to have unlimited liability for the shareholders (later on, by the revised law of 1864, a secondary class of shareholders with limited liability, en commandite, was allowed). Perhaps in consequence, or because "the development of the country did not call very urgently for a widespread system of bank offices at that time" (Flux, 1911, p. 32), these enskilda banks were slow to become established, the first charter being granted in 1830. Five more enskilda banks were started in the 1830s, two more in the late 1840s, and four more in the mid-1850s. From the start, the enskilda banks grew at a more rapid pace than the Riksbank. From 1834 to 1850, the loans and discounts of the enskilda banks grew by 16 mn dalers, while those of the Riksbank grew by $8\frac{1}{2}$ mn dalers (Flux, 1911, p. 32). Initially the funds of the enskilda banks, like those of the Riksbank, were primarily provided by note issue; thus in 1847 the enskilda banks had notes in circulation of $16\frac{1}{4}$ mn dalers and deposits and current account balances of $1\frac{2}{3}$ mn dalers (Flux, 1911, p. 40).

None of the earlier banks developed much of a deposit business (Flux, 1911, p. 53). That was to change in the latter part of the century. First, the Stockholm Enskilda Bank (most of the other earlier enskilda banks having been set up in other centers, thus avoiding close proximity and competition with the Riksbank) was set up in 1856 primarily to develop deposit banking (Flux, 1911, p. 53). Second, following the 1848 Act, which allowed for the establishment of joint stock companies, joint stock banks, with limited liability for all shareholders but without the right of note issue,[7] were founded; the first was established at Gothenburg in 1863. These joint stock banks grew rapidly in number and in size, there being 28 large joint stock banks (with capital over 1 mn kronor) and 12 smaller in 1908 (Flux, 1911, pp. 104–105).

Thus by the end of the nineteenth century there were three classes of banks in Sweden: the Riksbank, owned by Parliament (though not a state bank), with a traditional position as primary note issuer; the enskilda banks, with unlimited liability for ordinary shareholders and the right of note issue, but which after 1856 had also developed deposit banking; and the joint stock banks of limited liability, which concentrated on ordinary deposit business. The particular interest that this mix holds for monetary theorists and historians is that it provides an example of relatively free competition between ordinary commercial banks (the enskilda banks) and a publicly owned bank (the Riksbank) in the provision of notes.

By most market tests, the private sector, enskilda banks won this competition. Thus in 1840 the enskilda bank notes in issue amounted to 10 mn dalers, while the Riksbank had 41 mn in circulation (Flux, 1911, p. 30). By 1898 the note issue of the enskilda banks had risen to 79 mn kronor, while that of the Riksbank amounted to 71 mn kronor, (Flux, 1911, p. 90). Meanwhile, following a parliamentary decision in 1850/51, it was decided to set up subsidiary discount banks, called district banks, without note-issuing rights, to be established with private capital, but subordinate to and supported by subsidized loans from the Riksbank, specifically to provide competition with the enskilda banks (Flux, 1911, p. 43). They did not, however, establish strong local roots, obtaining only small amounts of capital and deposits, and lived instead off their subsidized loans from the Riksbank (Flux, 1911, pp. 43–49). This became too expensive, and this support was withdrawn by parliamentary resolution in 1862/63, "a step which inevitably led to the gradual extinction of the district banks" (Flux, 1911, p. 43). The enskilda banks meanwhile prospered despite some hostility on the part of the Riksbank; thus only from 1869 onward did the Riksbank accept their notes in payments (Flux, 1911, p. 65). Although there was some criticism that the fluctuations of note issue by the enskilda banks did not meet the needs of trade (Flux, 1911, p. 50), there were apparently no crises of confidence and bank failures that threw doubt upon the value of the privately issued currencies—perhaps in part because of the legislative control over the required backing for the note issue (e.g., in the 1864 law) and in the supervision carried out by the department of finance, with "the appointment of a special officer called the inspector of banks, in 1877"[8] (Flux, 1911, p. 64).

There was a considerable body of opinion in favor of free banking in Sweden. Thus, in 1864, "Among the influences tending to secure a prolongation of all essential privileges to the enskilda banks may be counted a mistrust, even among some who were not very friendly to the enskilda banks, of monopolistic power in the hands of the bank which was controlled by the legislative body" (Flux, 1911, p. 58). Earlier, a committee had advocated splitting the Riksbank into two departments, along the lines of the 1844 Bank of England Act, by which only the issue department would remain under full parliamentary control, while the banking department would involve private capital and be run as an ordinary competitive bank; the proposal was not accepted, but did influence thinking (Flux, 1911, p. 82).[9]

The comparative success of the enskilda banks in competition with the Riksbank in the provision of notes did not, however, necessarily simply reflect their greater efficiency. The public role of the Riksbank, and its constitution, limited its ability to compete on an equal basis. For example, as the ultimate guardian of the metallic reserves of the country, the Riksbank was required to hold a much higher cash reserve (Flux, 1911, p. 80).

Thus in 1898 the Riksbank held 31 mn kronor in gold, out of total gold held in the banking system of 40 mn kronor (Flux, 1911, p. 90); when the fiduciary limit was reached, the bank could only issue additional notes against specie or foreign exchange bills, e.g., drawn on Hamburg[10] (later London and Berlin also). The bank did not, at least for much of the period, pay interest on deposit (Flux, 1911, pp. 80–81) and so did not supplement its note-issuing functions with the broader deposit banking operations carried out by the enskilda banks after 1856. On the other hand, the Riksbank did not limit its assets solely to high-grade commercial paper, as did many of the other Central Banks, but used its capital, at least, to extend loans, often of an illiquid nature, a feature criticized by Flux, (1911, pp. 81, 88).

Nevertheless, in view of the comparative competitive success of the enskilda banks, it comes almost as a surprise to find that, under the law of 1897, Parliament agreed to centralize the note issue— after a transitional period—in the sole hands of the Riksbank. Flux is explicit about the form of the act and the mechanisms involved in the transfer of issue. He is, unfortunately, reticent about the reasons for the change, which is a question of some interest, since it brought to an end a period, unusual in monetary history, of free competition between private and publicly owned note-issuing banks. Perhaps the desire to centralize, strengthen, and protect and to have the gold reserves of the country under close central control formed one line of argument. Another reason could have been the desire to obtain a larger proportion of the profits of seignorage for the state. No doubt the fashion of developments elsewhere in Europe played a role.

What is clear in Flux's account is why the enskilda banks gave up their right of note issue. It was the usual combination of stick and carrot. The stick was the threat of higher tax on note issues: "It is clear that the banks, in accepting the terms offered for conceding the monopoly of note issue to the Riksbank, could not but be influenced by the knowledge that their gains from the note issues could be absorbed by the State by the simple process of raising the rate of this tax. They chose rather to be bought out than taxed out of their privileges" (Flux, 1911, p. 77). The carrot was the offer of loans, for a period of years, at subsidized rates from the Riksbank to replace the funds lost by the withdrawal of their notes (Flux, 1911, pp. 91–94). Moreover, the assumption of monopoly right to note issue by the Riksbank was accompanied ". . . by a stricter regulation of the nature of the business conducted by the central institution. The purpose directly in view was, doubtless, the more effective guarantee of the solidity and realizability of the assets of the note-issuing authority. Incidentally, however, it resigned to other institutions certain classes of business, and . . . the competition of the privileged central institution is removed" (Flux, 1911, pp. 94–95).

The above account indicates that there are a number of aspects of Swedish banking history of theoretical and practical interest; nevertheless, despite its long history as the main, publicly owned bank of the country, the Riksbank had not developed many of the chief features of a true Central Bank by the beginning of the twentieth century. There are virtually no indications of the Riksbank having adopted any part of the micro functions of providing support and insurance to individual banks and intermediaries, or of seeking to regulate and supervise the banks. Instead, regulation was achieved through legislation, supervised through bank inspectors provided by the Department of Finance.

As for conducting the macro function of managing overall monetary conditions, the bank did adopt responsibility for maintaining convertibility, first into silver after 1834 and then into gold after 1873, but only within the confines of its constitutional requirements. In the crises of 1857 and 1907/08 much of the pressure was relieved by the proceeds of a state loan made abroad being deposited with the Riksbank (Flux, 1911, pp. 82, 128). In 1869/70, the Riksbank allowed the note issue to exceed its legal maximum. What is notably missing from Flux's account of Riksbank operations, prior to 1903, when it assumed monopoly control over the note issue, is any report of the bank seeking to manage and control the level of money market interest rates in Sweden. It is notable that Flux criticizes the Riksbank even after 1903—in the crisis of 1907/08— for being slow to raise its discount rate, in order to protect the gold reserve, and even possibly for taking steps to preserve its own position by being slightly more restrictive in accommodating the needs of the rest of the Swedish banking system (Flux, 1911, pp. 127–128).[11]

Overall, the oldest established public bank was somewhat behindhand in developing into the role of a Central Bank.

The Danish National Bank

Flux (1911, pp. 123–147) also recounts the history of the Danish National Bank. The early history of banking in Denmark was checkered. A private bank was founded by charter in 1736 with the right of note issue. With no limitations being placed on such notes, it issued so much that it was forced to suspend convertibility in 1745. In 1773, the bank was taken over by the state, but under pressure of war, especially in 1807–1814, the government "... had to rely very largely on the issue of notes for meeting its expenses" (Flux, 1911, p. 135); the notes became practically worthless, and the state bank was declared bankrupt in 1813 (one of the rare occasions of a state bank with monopoly control of note issue being declared bankrupt). This was replaced by a new state bank, the Rigsbank, in 1813. After the war it had no cash reserve, so it supported its notes, and promised their future redemption, by a lien on all real estate, in the form of an annual rent charge; the same approach was followed by the fledgling Bank of Norway in 1816 (Flux, 1911, p. 147); these measures may have provided the example for the adoption of the rentenmark in the monetary reorganization of the Reichsbank in the interwar period.

Furthermore, the tax on large property holders formed the basis for the transformation of the Rigsbank into the privately owned National Bank in 1818, for the proprietors subject to tax became simply translated into shareholders. Once again, the translation of a state bank into a private bank is historically unusual,[1] though it was also considered in Sweden.

There were no other banks in Denmark until 1846, but thereafter, in the absence of any banking legislation, except that involving the one bank with monopoly right of note issue (as was also the case in Norway—Flux, 1911, p. 150), the growth of deposit banks—without the right of note issue—was rapid, 133 being in existence in 1909.

In 1908, however, there was a speculative banking crisis. "To alleviate in some degree the resulting distress, the Government came to the aid of the banks, establishing an advisory committee and providing a substantial fund to guarantee the creditors of the insolvent institutions." This is a further example of government, rather than the Central Bank, carrying out Central Bank-type micro functions.

As for the macro functions, the National Bank struggled hard to limit note issue and restore convertibility, which it finally attained in 1845. The hundred years, 1745–1845, of inconvertibility must represent some kind of record. Thereafter strict regulations on note issue enabled convertibility to be maintained, but some elasticity was provided by allowing the bank to exceed the maximum for a month before incurring penalties (utilized in October 1907) and, after 1907, to exceed the maximum on payment of a 5% tax (Flux, 1911, p. 143). Flux makes no mention, once again, of any efforts by the National Bank to control the level of money market interest rates, or monetary conditions more generally, so the extent, if any, to which the National Bank had assumed any macro functions of control by 1910, beyond the maintenance of the convertibility of its notes into gold, is uncertain.

Banca d'Italia

The origins of the Banca d'Italia, established as a result of a merger of existing banks in 1893, go back to 1844, when the Sardinian government "... sanctioned the foundation in Genoa of a discount and deposit bank having the privilege of issuing notes."[1] This bank merged in 1849 with a similar institution founded in Turin in 1847 to become the Banca Nazionale.

As the unification of Italy proceeded, this bank became the government's bank, providing large loans to the government, in return for which the government in 1866 freed it "... from the obligation of redeeming notes in specie by proclaiming the forced currency of the bank notes."[2] As additional provinces, e.g., Venice, became part of the Italian state, the Banca Nazionale absorbed other banks, in Parma, Bologna, and Venice, and became the largest note issuing bank in Italy.

Even so, the prior political fragmentation of Italy left the country at the beginning of the 1870s with "... conditions of the institutions of issue and the paper currency [that were] abnormal and unorganized, since there was a mixture of institutions, different in nature and privilege, and a hybrid circulation, partly private and partly belonging to the State, which could not truly serve the economic and monetary conditions of the country."[3] Indeed anyone could freely issue notes: "The law of 1874 was intended especially to regulate the monetary situation in Italy because everybody was issuing 'notes', even individuals and commercial firms; the country was overrun with little notes of 50, 25 and 20 centimes issued by everyone who liked to do so."[4]

The law of 1874 was, indeed, intended to reform and to regulate the monetary situation, but did not succeed notably well in that endeavor. Despite unification, regional loyalties remained strong. Rather than create a single central bank of issue, the government proclaimed an association, or consortium, of six banks of issue, though the Banca Nazionale was by far the largest.[5] The others were the Banca Nazionale Toscana, the Banca Toscana di Credito, Banca Romana, Banco di Napoli, and the Banco di Sicilia. Furthermore, the government seized the occasion to require the six banks "... to furnish the Government 1,000,000,000 lire in [small] notes."[6] These were to be forced currency. The notes to be issued, in larger denominations, by the banks for themselves were to be legal tender, but redeemable. They could, however, be redeemed either in specie or in the notes issued by the government. So, naturally, as long as the notes issued by the government were irredeemable, so also effectively were those issued by the association of note-issuing banks. Limits were placed on the notes issued by the banks for themselves: such notes were only to be issued up to three times capital and/or three times the reserve of specie, except that a provision for exceptional increases at times of "... urgent need" with the profits "... to accrue entirely to the State" was inserted.[7] A further safeguard against overissue was provided by an article requiring the mutual redemption of notes.

Initially the new system appeared to work well. Indeed, the incoming leftist government was able in 1881 to end the forced currency status of the Italian currency, which was considered "... a dishonor."[8] The finance minister, Magliani, arranged a massive foreign loan payable in gold of 644,000,000 lire, largely raised in London under the auspices of Hambro & Co. and Baring Bros.[9] This enabled the government to abolish forced currency and return to a metallic standard.

The weakness of the Italian monetary system lay in the plurality of banks of issue, and the competition between them to increase their size and profits. "It was at this period [1883–1885] that a lively competition arose between the Italian banks of issue, which carried them beyond the bounds to which they should have limited their activity, and had serious consequences for all, showing one of the most dangerous sides of the plurality of banks of issue.... Between the desire to rival the Bank of Naples, especially in the south of Italy, and that of not seeming to diminish dividends, the business of the Banca Nazionale became more active and apparently more profitable."[10] Thereafter, in the years 1885–1893, matters went from bad to worse, a thoroughly discreditable period in monetary history. There were two main economic problems. First, as a result of growing competition from North American agricultural products, the prosperity of Italian agriculture, especially in the South, suffered. Second, partly owing to improvident bank lending, a building boom, centered in Rome and Naples, took place, and then broke. These two developments left all the main banks with loans, initially often in the form of commercial bills, which could not be paid. Rather than declare these bad debts, the banks transformed such short-term loans into longer term mortgages, and established "credit foncier" mortgage subsidiaries, to which they transferred these mortgages, as well as making additional mortgages. These were financed by the issue of bonds and by loans from the main bank.[11]

Moreover, there was a rotten apple among the six banks of the association, i.e., the Banca Romana. This bank originated in 1850 when a papal decree founded the Banca dello Stato Pontifico. "From the start the Banca dello Stato Pontifico distinguished itself for the recklessness with which it committed abuses of all kinds."[12] It was bankrupt by 1870 (with known losses of 9,000,000 lire relative to capital of 3,000,000 lire),[13] but for political reasons, as it was the only bank in the papal states annexed to Italy in 1870, it was not liquidated or merged, but reorganized as the Banca Romana. It did not change its ways. "The institution which was economically and morally most corrupt was the Banca Romana, which, ill conducted under the papal administration, had not had a sound existence under the national Government, and was the veritable poison of Italian credit."[14]

It became deeply involved in the building boom in Rome, and effectively became bankrupt again when that collapsed. Although its weakness became increasingly evident, it fought to maintain its position and was supported on political grounds—e.g., the only indigenous bank of Rome, supporting employment in Rome and threatened by competition from outside banks.[15] Indeed, the authorities conspired to prop up the bank, and to keep silent about its state. Thus the government had ordered an inspection of the banks of issue in 1888 and found a cash deficit of 8,000,000 lire. The audit was suspended; the governor of the Banca Romana borrowed the money from the director general of the Banca Nazionale; the audit was reconvened and "the cash was found to be correct."[16]

It was impossible, however, to keep rumors of the condition of the bank from the public. That, together with the overexpansion of the bank's loans, meant that the Banca Romana began to suffer an increasingly adverse balance at the mutual redemption of notes, from 1887 onward. The bank then campaigned to be relieved of this redemption obligation. The government, again for political reasons, not only allowed this to occur covertly but actually absolved it from any obligation to redeem its notes in August 1891, while the Banca Nazionale made, in effect, large loans to the Banca Romana by withholding its notes from payment: "... the Banca Romana, which was already in a disastrous state, went headlong on the road to ruin."[17]

The plug was finally pulled by an economist, Maffeo Pantaleoni, who obtained a copy of the report of the inspection of the Banca Romana, completed in 1889—which had been hushed up—and made it public[18] in 1893. The result was an uproar in Parliament, the collapse and liquidation of the Banca Romana, and a new banking act, of August 1893. It might be thought that the problems and disadvantages of having a plurality of competing banks of issue would have been so obvious that the previous situation would not have been allowed to continue. Nonetheless, the power of regional interests remained so strong that despite the merger of the Banca Nazionale with the two Tuscan banks of issue, to form the Banca d'Italia (and requiring the Banca d'Italia to act as liquidator for the Banca Romana), the Banco di Napoli and Banco di Sicilia were retained as separate banks of issue. Although separate, the two regional banks were not really independent, since the law of 1893 effectively required them to work in tandem with the Banca d'Italia, the leading institution.[19] When asked, "Does the Bank of Italy, in fact, control the whole?" Canovai, the chief general secretary of the Banca d'Italia, replied, "Yes; in principle I have never approved the plurality of issuing banks."[20]

Besides the building boom and bust, and the agricultural difficulties, the 1893 crisis was also associated with a worsening government fiscal position, as military expenditures and expenditure on railroads led to a deficit, and a reduction in the specie reserve of the Treasury, as well as a weakening in the reserves of the banks. The crisis of 1893 drove Italy from its fixed exchange rate with France; its floating rate then depreciated, and the banks' notes were treated as legal tender, a forced currency.[21]

The financial crisis of 1893 was such a shock that it took a considerable time for the system to recover. All the remaining banks of issue were revealed to have massive bad debts, mostly concentrated in their credit foncier subsidiaries. The Banco di Napoli and the Banco di Sicilia were made public autonomous credit institutions under the supervision of the government. In fact, the Banco di Napoli was probably bankrupt in the years immediately after 1893, but the authorities kept it going; all its earnings were required to be retained and added to capital for fifteen years, from 1893 to 1908, as was also the case with the Banco di Sicilia.[22] The Banca d'Italia retained its status as a private joint stock bank, with the superior council elected primarily by shareholders and the director-general by the superior council.[23] However, the losses made at this period required the Banca d'Italia to call additional funds from shareholders and to write down the nominal value of existing capital.[24]

After the disastrous experiences leading up to the 1893 crisis, the Banking Act of 1893 was much stricter in defining the permissible operations, and the form of loans and assets, that the note-issuing banks could undertake. They were required to run off their now nonlegal mortgage operations with all due speed. A central bureau of supervision of the note-issuing banks under an inspector general was established in the Ministry of Finance: an inspector attended all council meetings of these banks and he, or the minister, could veto any acts regarded by them as ultra vires.[25]

The act provided that each note-issuing bank should have a maximum fiduciary issue, in relation to its capital, with a metallic reserve (as from 1894) of 40%, but could issue additional notes on a one-for-one basis that were backed by additional specie holdings. They could exceed the maximum at times of urgent need, but were subject to a special tax on the excess.[26]

The most unusual constraint on the freedom of operation of the Banca d'Italia was that the government, not the Bank, set the official discount rate. "The minimum rate of discount was to be fixed every three months by the decree of the minister of the Treasury and could not go below $3\frac{1}{2}$ per cent."[27] This applied commonly to all three banks of issue. They were also empowered to discount at 1% below discount rate to various savings and other "popular" banks; and they did have the discretion to discount high quality commercial paper below the official discount rate, with a minimum of 3%, "when the aggregate circulation of notes is below the normal maximum."[28]

This latter privilege was probably used more in the North because, despite the establishment of the Banca d'Italia, there remained regional differences in interest rates; thus "... the official rate of 5 per cent, which represents an average price of money in the greater part of southern Italy, a region less fully provided with available capital, proves in normal times high in central Italy and even higher in northern Italy."[29]

In the event, the official discount rate was held stable throughout the period, and despite (perhaps because of) the assumption by the government of responsibility for managing the level of official interest rates, economic and financial conditions recovered from the collapse of the early 1890s and blossomed in the 1900s. The state budget moved into surplus in 1898; the exchange rate against the French franc returned to parity in 1902 and stayed at par (indeed, the interesting question is why the authorities did *not* choose to restore convertibility, but rolled onward the legal tender status of the notes of the banks of issue year by year); there was a successful conversion issue, reducing the coupon on Italian rentes in 1906; the banking system easily weathered the crisis of 1907, which was not severe in Italy; the balance of payments strengthened, with Italy becoming a creditor nation; and economic activity generally did well.[30]

With the improvement in economic and financial conditions, the Banca d'Italia (and the other two banks of issue) were able to add massively to their metallic reserves.[31] This provided them with considerable leeway (under the maxima legally permitted) to vary their note issue in accordance with the needs of trade, at the officially established discount rate; only in some of the earlier years, e.g., in the expansion of discounts and note issue from 1897 to 1899, did such accommodation appear to provide any threat to financial stability.[32] What is less clear is whether the accumulation of (barren) metallic reserves in the Banca d'Italia (the other two banks of issue being public autonomous bodies) caused the council to feel any conflict of interest between its obligation to the shareholders and the objective of maintaining financial stability. Probably a combination of legal constraints over interest rates and permissible business, the removal of competitive commercial pressures in 1893, and memories of the losses caused by the earlier disastrous events reduced the potential for such conflicts of interest.

As has been demonstrated (see note 31), the banks of issue had relatively few deposit liabilities, the bulk of their funds coming from note issue. This may have been partly owing to the constraints under which they operated. Thus, there were limits on the interest rates that they could offer on demand deposits, and, like the fiduciary note issue, they had to be covered by a 40% cash reserve ratio.[33] Nevertheless, it is not clear from the reports available to the National Monetary Commission whether deposit banking was being undertaken on any large scale elsewhere, or was still relatively underdeveloped, in Italy at this time (1910).

The main deposit banks were the credit societies, of which the largest were the Banca Commerciale Italiana, Credito Italiano, Banco di Roma, and Societa Bancaria Italiana, but, apart from reporting the size of their capital,[34] there is little record in these sources of their size or development. In addition, there were certain mortgage and other credit institutions, such as the Monte dei Paschi di Siena, and a wide range of other, generally small, private savings banks, popular and cooperative credit banks, postal savings banks, etc.[35] A somewhat fuller account of the structure and development of the Italian banking system during these years is provided by Cohen (1972).

What was again unusual in Italy was that "private banks do not keep their reserve with the Bank of Italy"; instead, they kept "... their own stock of money."[36] Although the Banca d'Italia did not, therefore, normally act as a bankers' bank, nevertheless, over the course of the years it did provide lender of last resort services to the Italian banking system. Canovai, for example, having noted that the private banks did not keep reserves there, went on to note that "it is only when the resources of the private banks are exhausted and they need money that they go to the issue banks" (*European Interviews*, p. 527), which they obtained by rediscounting. Events were such as to give the Banca d'Italia experience with this role.

Indeed, the lender of last resort role had been assumed even earlier by the Banca Nazionale before the 1893 merger. The support of the Banca Nazionale for the Banca Romana has already been noted.[37] In addition, in 1889 the Banca Nazionale provided assistance to the Banca Tiberina, the Compagnia Fondiaria Italiana, and others, in order to stem a banking crisis in Turin. Canovai quotes extensively from the report to the shareholders on the operations of the year 1889 of the general director of the Banca Nazionale. This statement makes its abundantly clear that the bank, supported and prompted by the government, was sensible of, and assumed, the duties of a lender of last resort.[38]

Indeed, shortly after the crisis of 1893 and the passing of the Banking Act of August 1893, there was a secondary crisis, arising from the decline in the value of Italian rentes in Paris and falls in Italian Stock Exchange values, that dragged down the Credito Mobiliare Italiano and the Banca Generale. The government had to relax temporarily the limitations on note issue and reserves just enacted, in order to relieve the pressures, but, even so, both institutions went into forced liquidation.[39] Finally, in 1905/06, certain banks, having become involved in industrial finance, were adversely affected by speculative fluctuations in Stock Exchange prices. The Societa Bancaria Italiana got into serious difficulties: the Banca d'Italia not only provided direct help itself, but managed to arrange some contribution from other banks, and succeeded in saving, and then reconstructing, the Societa[40]—on this also see Cohen (1972, pp. 83–84).

Canovai claimed that

> this assistance, very different from the forms of aid that had been afforded twenty years before [referring probably to the support for the Banca Romana], showed how effective a safeguard for a country is the existence of a great bank of issue in moments of difficulty and disturbance; and it showed further that the most difficult ordeals can be surmounted and the most severe disasters avoided by comparatively insignificant means, when there is no lack of precise perception of the situation and promptness in meeting it.[41]

Despite not acting in a day-to-day capacity as a bankers' bank, by the start of the twentieth century the Banca d'Italia had considerable experience and appreciation of the micro functions of a Central Bank. On the other hand, the legacy of political separation and regional sensitivities, the unhappy experience of the association of a plurality of banks of issue (1874–1893), and the close direction of the government thereafter meant that the Banca d'Italia remained largely unfledged in carrying out the macro functions of a Central Bank prior to World War I.

The Austro-Hungarian Bank

The study of the Austro-Hungarian Bank in the papers collected for the National Monetary Commission (NMC) is quite short and less than fully satisfactory. Indeed the paper by Prof. Zuckerkandl was not specially commissioned by the NMC itself, but was lifted from Conrad's *Handworterbuch der Staatswissenschaften*, third edition. The study is particularly incomplete in that it makes virtually no reference to the development of other banks, or financial intermediaries, within the Austro-Hungarian empire, and *no* description whatsoever of any relationship between the Austro-Hungarian Bank and other banks in the twin monarchy, e.g., as the bankers' bank or lender-of-last-resort. The Austro-Hungarian Bank itself was primarily a note-issuing bank, having comparatively only few deposits.[1] Whether commercial deposit banking was developing at the same time in Austro-Hungary is not revealed in this source. Anyhow there is no account here of the Bank taking on any part of the micro functions of Central Banking in a relationship with other banks.

Instead, Prof. Zuckerkandl's account concentrates on the long, close, complex (and somewhat depressing) relationship between the Bank and the government. The Bank originated in 1816 as the Chartered Austrian National Bank. It was established by the government primarily for the purpose of reorganizing and rehabilitating the currency system of the country, following the financial disturbances of the Napoleonic wars and the issue of large volumes of government forced currency paper, which depreciated heavily against silver. The public was invited to exchange depreciated government paper in exchange for bonds (interest to be paid in silver coin), bank shares, and bank notes (to be redeemable in silver): the government transferred bonds and silver to the bank in exchange for its canceled notes. In the event, the terms for the swap were made too generous; the public bought bonds and bank notes with government paper, and then sought to exercise its right to convert the bank notes into silver. This put pressure on the Bank's silver reserves, and convertibility was restricted.[2]

Besides its holdings of government bonds, arising from the attempted redemption, the Bank was intended to undertake ordinary (commercial) discount business "... and eventually the granting of credit on mortgage."[3] Following further fiscal problems connected with military expenditures in Italy, however, a large, but hidden, proportion of the discounts were, in fact, government drafts. The Bank was not required to maintain any required reserve ratio, and this varied largely in response to pressures from the government for finance. This made the Bank highly profitable,[4] but left its balance sheet in a dangerously exposed state. This latter was kept hidden by pervasive secrecy: thus "... the statements regarding the condition of the bank ... were withheld even from the committee of the bank, remaining a bureaucratic secret of the directors and a few individuals connected with the bank and the finance administration."[5]

The risky balance sheet, high profits, and pervasive secrecy were not due to commercial pressures for profit maximization. The Bank had a practical monopoly, though not the legally exclusive privilege, of note issue,[6] and was always in practice subject to government control, even though the Bank was owned by private shareholders. Although they chose the directors, the governor and his deputy were appointed by the government and there was also a government official, a "commissary" who sat in on board meetings, etc., and could overrule decisions on "public welfare" grounds.[7] Although most of the profits did accrue, in these earlier years, to the shareholders, the dividends were determined "... after a preliminary conference on the part of the managers with the ministry of finance."[8] Moreover, changes in the Bank's discount rate "... from 1829 on were made at the behest of the minister of finance."[9]

Despite this tight grip by the government on the operations of the Bank, there was some leeway for it to operate in a normal commercial manner. It did not make notably good use of such opportunities.

> Those who understood the precise import of the figures of the bank statements condemned the new way of carrying on the discount business, the more that they were convinced that the managers favored a few large commercial houses, that the purpose for which the bank notes were wanted was not scrutinized, and that the rate of discount was kept down purposely in order to benefit the large customers of the bank. In the new charter, that of July 1, 1841, virtually the entire management of the bank was placed under the control of the ministry of finance.[10]

Worse was to befall the Bank and the financial system. From 1848 till 1873 a series of shocks occurred: first, the 1848 political disturbances and the war in Italy, then the Eastern war in 1854, then the further war in Italy in 1859, then the Austro-Prussian War of 1866, and finally the financial crash of 1873. In each case (except the last), the government was forced to borrow massively from the Bank, often issued its own inconvertible paper, and the Bank's own notes were granted legal tender, a forced currency status. Following each of these shocks, the government tried to reorganize and re-establish convertibility and monetary rectitude by making large debt sales, using the proceeds, often via the National Bank, to redeem its own paper. Then, before it had succeeded, along came the next shock.[11]

Meanwhile, toward the end of these troubled years, the administration of the Bank was complicated by the 1867 Ausgleich, or union, between Austria and Hungary. Monetary arrangements necessarily formed part of the agreement, and one of the conditions, arrived at in 1867, was that the notes of the National Bank should be legal tender in Hungary also, and that the Bank ". . . be bound to establish branches in Hungary wherever the Government should deem it necessary, and to grant loans on the securities of both halves of the monarchy." However, "This agreement was not formally communicated to the bank until the beginning of 1870 [!]."[12] The "bank question" (two or one, division of control and responsibility of a single bank, etc.) then continued until (partially) settled by legislation in 1878, which reformed the Chartered Austrian National Bank as the Austro-Hungarian Bank, with a careful balancing of national interests—governor appointed on joint recommendation of Austrian and Hungarian ministers of finance, one deputy governor appointed by each, etc.—though ultimately there was an Austrian majority on the council, and the ratios of notes, government profit shares, etc., were generally 70 Austria to 30 Hungary.[13]

Despite the administrative complications that ensued from the need to be careful about national balance and sensitivities, the political and financial scene became less turbulent from the mid-1870s. Prior to the 1870s, Austria had been on a silver standard, but in 1871 and 1872 the National Bank switched much of its metallic reserves to gold. This had been a step envisaged for the Austro-Hungarian monarchy, ". . . according to the principles laid down at the Paris monetary conference,"[14] but the main impetus came from the Bank's "pessimistic view" of future silver prices.[15] There then followed an interregnum of about twenty years, during which the country was on a limping silver standard, having signaled an intention to shift to a Gold Standard. This, on occasion, allowed arbitrageurs to obtain profits by bringing in silver for coinage.[16] In

1892, however, the government effectively moved onto a Gold Standard, though the final consummation was set for the beginning of 1900.[17] The period of stability, which allowed the country to join the Gold Standard, also enabled the government finally to succeed in redeeming its various tranches of paper in the years 1899–1900: "The obligation to accept government notes in payment of debt terminated in 1903."[18]

By the turn of the century, the finances of the monarchy had fully recovered from the earlier (1848–1873) period of disturbance. The main (macro-economic) concern of the Austro-Hungarian Bank thenceforth was the maintenance of the exchange rate. "The activity of the bank in this direction is directed toward the steadying of the foreign exchanges and the maintenance of the relative values of the crown (the unit of the Austro-Hungarian gold standard) and the standard gold coins of other countries, as established in 1892."[19]

For this function Zuckerkandl notes that the central bank "... is not supposed to act ... as an institution organized for profit, but as an organ of the Government," and should operate "... not for the sake of profit, but solely in the interest of the public."[20] It was clearly appreciated that in its major macro-economic role the Central Bank should eschew profit maximization.[21] This self-denial was, perhaps, easier to bear for the shareholders, since the larger share (2/3) of any excess profits now went to the government anyhow.[22]

The Austro-Hungarian Bank sought to reinforce its gold holdings by the standard Central Bank tricks—e.g., paying a relatively high market rate for gold and making advances at zero interest to gold importers[23]—but its usual defense against adverse movements in the exchanges was to deploy large holdings of foreign bills of exchange as a form of buffer stock.[24] Also, on the occasion of the second charter of the Austro-Hungarian Bank (1887), the opportunity was taken to provide for additional note issue (beyond that permissible through specie holdings and normal fiduciary issue), at times of emergency, on payment of 5% tax on the excess, along the lines pioneered by the Reichsbank. Nevertheless, despite these preliminary lines of defense, the ultimate protection for the reserves lay in the Central Bank's ability to vary market interest rates for this purpose. This was used, for example, for the increase from 5% to 6% in November 1907.

Nevertheless there were still some questions about the Bank's ability to control short-term market rates effectively under all circumstances. Thus the Bank "... repeatedly represented to the two governments the desirability of having the free cash of the central government treasuries transferred to its vaults in order that it might exercise a greater influence on the domestic money market." [25] Before 1901, the specie accruing to the treasuries had been "... deposited with private bankers, who allowed a low rate of interest," but by agreement in 1901 the governments agreed to centralize their gold holdings with the Bank, and "... to effect their international payments through its channels." [26] In return, the Bank contracted to pay interest on such deposits: it had, earlier in 1894, been authorized, through a change in its statutes, "... to open interest-bearing accounts so as to enable it in case of need to draw money from abroad by the payment of interest in place of putting up the rate of discount." [27]

The relationship of the Bank and the government remained close throughout the period; the extent to which either the initiative or the decision to change the rate of discount lay with the Bank or with the ministers of finance is unclear from Zuckerkandl's account. The degree of formal control did vary somewhat from period to period. As already noted, in 1841 the Bank was virtually "... placed under the control of the ministry of finance." That did not prevent "much favoritism [being] shown in the granting of credit," [28] and, following "the installation in 1861 of a national parliament," [29] a new law was passed in 1862 giving a larger role to the private shareholders in the Bank's affairs. Indeed, the general assembly was to choose a committee of twelve members, who even "... were to have a voice in deliberations relative to changes in the rate of interest," and the direct control of the state over the Bank was lessened.[30] The pendulum swung back in 1899, on the occasion of a further renewal of the Bank's charter, when "the governmental control over the management of the bank was extended in various ways." [31]

Of all the European central banks considered here (excluding Russia), the Austro-Hungarian Bank during these years (circa 1890–

1910) appeared most under the thumb of the government. This may have helped to facilitate its adoption of a non-profit-maximizing role in undertaking its macro-economic function (primarily of maintaining the exchange rate at its Gold Standard parity). In addition, the Bank helped to develop certain giro payments functions, in competition with the postal savings bank, initially largely on behalf of the government,[32] and its offices grew from 50 in 1880 to 254 in 1907, evenly spread between Austria and Hungary,[33] so it had begun to play a direct part in improving the payments transmission mechanism. Apart from that, as earlier noted, there is no mention in Zuckerkandl's paper of the Bank playing any part in the micro function of supporting and sustaining the private commercial banking sector.

A more recent paper on the interrelationship between banking and economic development in Austria, by Rudolph (1972), also has little to say on the relationship between the Bank and the banks. Rudolph writes (1972, p. 32) that "in effect, the bank served only the government and several of the large private houses...." This passage only dealt with the period 1800–1848, but there was no subsequent reference to the Bank in the sections dealing with later developments, e.g., the formation in the 1850s, and subsequent operations of the joint-stock credit institutions.

The National Bank of Belgium

When the Japanese were searching for a model of a Central Bank to install in their own country, they took the National Bank of Belgium as their exemplar: also, "When the Government of Holland remodeled the charter of the Bank of the Netherlands in 1864, the new law was based upon that of Belgium."[1] It is not entirely clear from Conant's account (1911), however, what features of the operations of the Bank excited the admiration of contemporaries.

Probably the most remarkable aspect of its constitution was the extreme emphasis placed upon limiting the assets that it could hold to liquid, commercial paper.[2] This limitation reflected the history and circumstances of its foundation in 1850. When Belgium was separated from Holland in 1830, the main bank then operating was the Société Générale, which "... dated from early in the nineteenth century, and under the Dutch sovereignity performed most of the financial operations of the Government. The control of the institution was in the hands of the Dutch element, who felt little sympathy with the new political regime in Belgium." The new Belgian government initially continued to use the Société Générale as its bank, though the latter refused to accept any supervision from the government over its operations.[3] Not perhaps surprisingly, the government then supported the creation of a rival institution, the Bank of Belgium, in 1835, which was immediately allocated the role of banker to the government.[4]

The Bank of Belgium was, naturally, weaker than the Société Générale, and, at time of political dispute with Holland over the boundaries of Limbourg and Luxembourg, in 1838, the latter "... seized the occasion to cripple its younger rival by gathering up its notes and presenting them for redemption."[5] "The Bank of Belgium was forced to suspend and to seek the assistance of the Government,"[6] which was provided in the form of a large loan. The intense rivalry between these two main banking institutions was not the only source of fragility; both were also "industrial banks" and tied up a large proportion of their assets in company promotions. While this form of banking is, no doubt, of considerable value in bringing forward industrial development,[7] not only are the assets illiquid, but also their value comes under suspicion and threat at times of financial stringency. Anyhow, whether or not the accusation was entirely valid, contemporaries attributed the continuing financial problems in Belgium, 1839–1848, largely to the fact that both the Société Générale and the Bank of Belgium tried to combine the roles of bank of issue and industrial bank.

Anyhow, despite having been bailed out by the government in 1839, the Bank of Belgium was forced temporarily to suspend convertibility again in 1842, and relinquished its role as cashier to the government. The Société Générale was also adversely affected, and had to shut most of its branches, but managed to come through the difficulties, and resumed the role of banker to the government, since no other bank could fulfil the role. In the crisis of 1848 both banks had again to suspend payments. Their position was protected for the time being by declaring their notes legal tender (subject to a restriction on the amount of issue), but, following the 1842 crisis, "... those responsible for the conduct of public affairs were considering seriously the creation of an institution which should be restricted in the scope of its operations to commercial banking and should not be exposed, like the existing institutions, to the results of unsound financiering."[8] The crisis of 1848 gave the government "... an opportune occasion for putting its plans in execution,"[9] and the result was the establishment of the National Bank by the law of May 5, 1850.

This law required that "... no bank of issue shall be constituted by shares except under the form of a joint-stock company and by virtue of a law."[10] While this may have left open a loophole for individuals, and societies in a collective name, to open a bank of issue—and was expressly intended to allow the government to establish another competing bank, if felt necessary—in practice, the National Bank enjoyed a monopoly of note issue.[11] As already noted, a main feature of its constitution was the strict limitation on permissible assets, which was rigorously interpreted.[12] Otherwise, however, the volume of note issue was left largely unrestricted and flexible: "This issue is unlimited in amount and is not restricted by the charter even as to the proportion of cash reserve required to be held."[13]

This latter was left for agreement between the minister of finance and the Bank. Initially, the reserve ratio was fixed at 25% of all obligations payable on sight (both notes and current accounts), but was altered in 1872, at the time of the revision of the charter, to $33\frac{1}{3}\%$ "... but with authority to the ministry to suspend the requirement when it might be advisable."[14] Compared to its large note issues, the current accounts of the National Bank, which included, of course, the accounts held for the state,[15] were relatively small, about one-tenth of its total liabilities.[16] The comparatively small size of its deposits was due, in some large part, to its refusal to pay interest on them. Although this step greatly reduced the extent of competition with the Belgian joint stock banks, whose "... current accounts ... have increased enormously with the expansion of the business of the country, [while] the balance of such accounts at the

National Bank has remained comparatively stationary,"[17] the motive for adopting this restriction was different. It was apparently due to a theoretical distinction between the transaction functions of non-interest-bearing sight deposits, which were seen to be close substitutes for notes, and limited to operational needs, and so unlikely to be withdrawn, as compared and contrasted with the investment character of interest-bearing deposits, which would be a dangerous, and out-of-character, liability for bank of issue.[18]

The National Bank was described, in a report on the occasion of the renewal of its charter in 1900, as "the bank of bankers,"[19] but there is no mention in Conant's paper of the other banks holding large, stable, or any required deposit balances with the Bank. No doubt they held some balances with the Bank in order to facilitate payments. The Bank was required by the government to open agencies in all the major business centers in Belgium, and had 39 such agencies.[20] Although Conant makes no mention of a clearing-house, the provision of drafts[21] and the collection of checks across this agency network will have facilitated payments.

The other banks looked to their ability to discount paper with the National Bank, not to their deposits with it, as their main source of liquidity. Its domestic discounts were "... made up largely of redis-counts extended to the joint-stock and private banks, which have absorbed the bulk of the growth in deposit business...."[22] Certainly, there was no criticism of the National Bank from the rest of the financial community, e.g., at the time of the renewal of its charter in 1900; "On the contrary, the Union of Credit and the popular banks have inscribed in their reports the expression of their satisfaction and of their gratitude."[23]

Somewhat unusually, in addition to its ordinary functions as a Central Bank, the government also required the Bank to administer and operate the General Savings Bank,[24] though the latter, founded in 1865, was a separate financial entity. The Bank used some of these funds to finance the Credit Foncier, the Society of Working Men's Homes, and other building societies.[25]

Apart from such business relationships, there is only one reference in Conant's work of any more direct, or closer, relationship with the commercial banks, e.g., as lender-of-last-resort. Thus,

"Referring to the suspension of a banking house at Brussels a few years ago [before 1899], it was recounted how several millions had been obtained within an hour from the National Bank."[26]

It is not clear, however, whether the funds were supplied through discounts of acceptable commercial paper. Thus, it seems that, by 1910, the National Bank had not had much direct involvement, as lender-of-last-resort or in a supervisory mode, with the commercial banks in Belgium. The relatively placid nature of macro-financial developments in Belgium in the latter part of the nineteenth century may have helped in this respect.

The worst disturbance arose in 1870, and this was occasioned by a political crisis rather than by economic/financial problems. The 1870 Franco-Prussian War led to an increased demand for financial accommodation in the form of discounts at the National Bank. The natural nervousness, obviously shared by the politicians, was then worsened by acts by the Ministry of Finance, which required the transfer of the specie reserve from Brussels to Antwerp, and the Ministry of War, which gave instructions to its agents to exchange its existing holding of Bank notes into specie. Although this latter order was countermanded quickly, there was a run on the Bank, and it had to raise interest rates sharply, draw on its foreign bill holdings, restrict redemptions to its Brussels Head Office, etc.[27]

For the rest, the main macro-economic function of the Bank was the maintenance of convertibility. This exercise was more than a little complicated in Belgium by the nature of the bimetallic currency standard and the intricate relationships of the Latin Union. Nevertheless, the principles of the maintenance of convertibility remained the same. First, as in many other European Central Banks, the Bank's holdings of foreign bills of exchange, which could be included as part of the required reserve ratio (of $33\frac{1}{3}\%$ from 1872) and which formed "... about 25 per cent of the total computed reserve in 1900,"[28] were used as a buffer stock as a first line of defense against shocks. Thus in the 1870 crisis, holdings of 64 mn francs on July 21 were reduced to 7 mn francs by the end of July: in 1898, when other Central Banks posted higher interest rates, the National Bank was able to maintain its own rate constant by reducing its foreign bill portfolio from 123 mn francs to 98 mn francs.

But when such sources of temporary adjustment and flexibility were exhausted, the main instrument that the Bank could use to maintain financial equilibrium was its control over its discount rate.[29] The administrative council of the Bank had special concern for "... the rate on credits and advances, and discount affairs in general."[30] The Bank was privately owned, and the administrative boards and directors[31] were chosen by the shareholders, but the governor was appointed by the king.[32] It is not clear from Conant's account whether the governor would consult with the government at all before varying the discount rate, but the indications are that the initiative lay primarily, if not wholly, with the Bank.

The Bank was, however, somewhat reluctant to use this instrument, preferring to keep its discount rate low and stable. Its policy was described as midway between that of the Bank of England and that of the Banque de France.[33] It might be thought that the profit motive would encourage a privately owned bank of issue to raise its discount rate at times of pressure, but the reverse was true in this particular case. Among the arrangements that the government made to raise revenue from the privileged position of the National Bank was a law to extract all the excess earnings resulting from a discount rate above a certain level. "By the later law [of 1900] the Bank can not profit from a discount rate above $3\frac{1}{2}$ per cent. To the latter provision is attributed by some the disposition of the Bank in recent years to prefer to derive a profit from its note circulation, at the expense of unfavorable foreign exchanges, rather than to raise the discount rate radically in order to protect its gold reserve and the monetary stock of Belgium."[34]

It would appear that Conant himself was one of those who attributed the Bank's policy of keeping rates at a low, stable level, despite a generally unfavorable and weak exchange rate, to the profit motive, though he also notes that "... this policy [was] more beneficial to commercial interests and less likely to impair its own popularity than the drastic elevation of the discount rate which protects the reserve of the Bank of England."[35]

The interaction of this policy with the Belgian currency standard caused certain recurring problems. The weak exchange allowed arbitrage profits to be made on the export of silver coins from

Belgium[36] (primarily 5 Fr pieces); the silver coins of the Latin Union were acceptable in each others' countries, so a vast, though uncertain, volume of Belgian silver coin, whose specie value had fallen well below its fiat value—owing to the weakness of silver prices—was held outside Belgium, primarily in France. This implied a considerable contingent liability, which greatly exercised the Belgian authorities. This complex story is recounted at some length by Conant,[37] and represented, in his view, the main feature of "The Monetary Experience of Belgium." So the influence, such as it was, of profit incentives on the Bank in helping to cause this situation to occur was of some considerable importance.

The Bank of Japan

Although the Japanese looked to the West, following the Meiji Restoration in 1868, for examples to follow in industrial and financial development, they generally accommodated such Western institutions to Japanese practices. This is certainly the case with banking, notably including Central Banking. As recorded in the last section, on the National Bank of Belgium, the statutes of the Bank of Japan, founded 1882, were modeled on those of the National Bank, but the reality of operation became markedly different. Moreover, there had been an earlier attempt to reform the currency system by the introduction of a foreign system, with "national banks," whose structure was directly copied from US arrangements.[1] However,

> The initial experiments in institution-building reflected more a faith in the efficacy of Western financial institutions than an understanding of their appropriate operations.[2]
>
> As it was found, however, that such a [national bank] system did not work well on account of its being unsuitable to national conditions, the regulations were amended in 1876 and in 1882, when the central bank system was adopted.[3]

Opinions are somewhat divided on the conditions of the Japanese financial and banking system at the end of the Tokugawa Shogunate. Prime Minister Katsura described them as "primitive,"[4] but, perhaps, even by 1910, politicians and officials of the new Meiji regime might be tempted to denigrate the previous state of affairs. Patrick, on the other hand, records that "the Meiji economy inherited considerable financial expertise, though with a rather traditional, commercial orientation from the Tokugawa period,"[5] and is inclined to stress the indigenous development, e.g., of commercial bills, and the continuity of private banks and quasi banks.[6] Be that as it may, there was an incentive to the new Meiji government to establish a new banking system, in order to reform the currency system, involving by then rather a jumble of inconvertible government paper, specie, and other private paper, to provide a sounder basis for the government's own finance, and to foster the general development of banking.

As already noted, the first shot involved an attempt to replicate the US national bank system. The founders of such banks were to use 60% of their capital to acquire (inconvertible) government notes and to present these (for retirement) to the government, against which they would be allocated 6% government bonds, which in turn could be used as the backing for bank notes. The other 40% of their capital was to be held as a reserve in specie (silver at the time); since deposit banking was then comparatively new, i.e., most of the banks' liabilities took the form of notes rather than deposits, this represented a high required reserve ratio; moreover, with market interest rates usually over 10%, taking out notes on 6% bonds was hardly attractive.

In addition, further issues of government paper drove specie to a premium, encouraging bank note holders to redeem their notes in specie, and the government, in 1874, made some (destabilizing) changes in its arrangements for holding deposits at the national banks.[7] Not surprisingly, only four national banks were founded under this regime, and few such bank notes remained outstanding.

These arrangements were an obvious failure, and were comprehensively reformed in 1876. An additional incentive for the reform was the commutation of the hereditary pensions of the nobles (Kwazoku) and the gentry and samurai (Shizoku) into bonds in that same year: by encouraging banks to be formed with note issue backed by the bonds issued for that purpose, the government could maintain a market for this new, massive bond issue (thereby improving its uncertain political hold—the Satsuma rebellion occurred in 1877) and encourage banking development all at the same time.[8] Anyhow, conditions for note issue were made much more attractive; convertibility was now only required into inconvertible government paper; 80% of capital in the form of existing bonds could be used as backing for notes, with a 20% reserve (of government notes). This stimulated the establishment of a large number of such banks, 153 in all, and the government, fearing an excessive expansion of (inconvertible) notes, then stopped the formation of any more national banks.

It is, theoretically, possible that this latter, revised (1876), system of national banks could have endured. What it failed to do, however, was to provide sufficient centralized control over the currency, over foreign exchange and the financing of foreign trade, and over the banking system more generally and for the financial arrangements of the government. When Count Matsukata became minister of finance in 1881, having taken immediate steps to reduce the outstanding volume of government paper and its depreciation against silver, he next "... less than six months after entering his duties as minister of finance ... submitted a memorandum to the Government urging the establishment of a central bank."[9] "A central bank was, moreover, peculiarly in keeping with the general character of the government system of the country, the activities of which are to an unusual extent centralized in Tokyo."[10]

One of the main areas of concern for the Japanese monetary authorities was external finance; the trade account remained in persistant deficit, balanced by a capital inflow, and interest rates were considerably lower abroad than in Japan. In these circumstances the authorities were keen to stimulate exports, to support the domestic financing of foreign trade, and to organize international bond issues (notably at the time of the 1904/05 Russo-Japanese War), as well as to manage the foreign exchange market and to protect and sustain specie reserves (silver before 1897, after which date the Japanese joined the Gold Standard). In its external financing activities, the Bank of Japan worked with, and through, the Yokohama Specie Bank.

This was, in some large part, the result of historical accident. The Yokohama Specie Bank was founded first, in 1880, under private auspices, though with the support of the minister of finance, Marquis Okuma, to finance the traders in the port of Yokohama. The government initially "... provided one-third of the capital and up to three-quarters of the deposits. The bank suffered major losses in its early operations, and in the process of repeatedly bailing it out the government assumed complete control."[11] Once the Bank of Japan was established, the two worked in close conjunction.

> The Yokohama Specie Bank has very close relations with the Bank of Japan, the latter exercising strict supervision over the business of the former. Under the law the deputy governor of the Bank of Japan acts as governor of the Yokohama Specie Bank, and the deputy governor of the latter acts as director of the Bank of Japan. The Yokohama Bank is an organ of foreign exchange established to foster foreign trade and to absorb specie from abroad. For that purpose the Bank of Japan advances funds to the Yokohama Specie Bank at a specially low rate [2%], and also rediscounts bills at the request of the Specie Bank. The Bank of Japan never engages directly in foreign exchange or in sending money abroad. Government bonds abroad and receipts and disbursements of the Treasury funds abroad are managed by the Yokohama Specie Bank under the supervision of the Bank of Japan.[12]

Although the conduct of external finance, via the Yokohama Specie Bank, was peculiar to Japan, for the rest the Bank of Japan was, in form, modeled on the National Bank of Belgium. Thus Prime Minister Katsura stated that "after careful study and comparison of the central banking systems of Europe we found that ... in point of perfection of organization the Bank of Belgium was peerless ... consequently it was decided by Japan to adopt the Belgian system ... yet in note-issuing capacity and the rate of reserve a method resembling the German one was included,"[13] and that "its charter and by-laws were closely modeled upon those of the National Bank of Belgium."[14] Whatever the legal form may have been, however, the reality was that the Bank of Japan developed into a very different institution from the National Bank of Belgium.

Although the governor of the latter was appointed by the king, the role of the private shareholders, the independence of the Bank, and the inducements of the profit motive were important, as noted in the previous section, in the Belgian case. In Japan, however, the Bank was, from the outset, part of the governmental system, closely supervised by the Ministry of Finance.

> The govenor and vice-govenor are appointed by the government. The Bank is placed under several restrictions. The Government reserves the right to attach supervising officials, thus bringing the institution under the strictest government surveillance.[15]

> The relations between the Government and the Bank of Japan are of a very close character. When the latter was first established, the Government was a very large shareholder, but these shares were afterwards transferred to the Imperial Household Department.... The Government's supervision is very strict.[16]

> Any person desiring to become a shareholder of the Bank of Japan [must] obtain the permission of the Minister of Finance.... The Government superintends all the business of the Bank of Japan and restricts or forbids the acts of the Bank not conforming to the Bank's act or articles of association or contrary to the interests of the Government.[17]

> In fact, aside from emergencies, it is rather as an organ of the Government in relation both to the monetary system of the country, and the government finances that the Bank may be said to have rendered its greatest service and not as a part of the banking system of the country.[18]

> Perhaps because it was created, full blown, under the instigation and control of the Minister of Finance, rather than evolving, the Bank of Japan always remained rather subservient to the Treasury."[19]

It is, moreover, remarkable that the four papers on banking in Japan submitted to the National Monetary Commission made no mention at all of the profitability of the Bank of Japan, the division of its earnings between shareholders and the government, the role of private shareholders, etc. It was as if for all practical purposes the Bank of Japan functioned as a public sector non-profit-maximizing institution from the outset.

Meanwhile, the National Bank of Belgium dealt with the other banks in Belgium rather at arm's length, primarily through discounting their bills, in the same way as it discounted any acceptable bills, through the market—there was no indication in Conant's account of any closer involvement. In complete contrast, the Bank of Japan became directly and closely involved in direct support of the Japanese banking system. Indeed, rather than deal with all purveyors of acceptable paper at market rates (or above), the Bank of Japan dealt primarily with (a few large) banks, generally at a below market, subsidized rate. The key feature of the National Bank of Belgium was that it restricted its assets to liquid, commercial paper; the Bank of Japan lent directly to banks on the basis of relatively illiquid stocks as collateral security.

Thus:

> The Bank of Japan, since its establishment, has made a practice of aiding the ordinary banks, and there exists a considerable gulf between its interest rate and that of ordinary banks—that is, the discount rate of the Bank of Japan is, as a rule, much lower than that of ordinary banks.[20]

> Until 1897 the Bank confined its lending operations entirely to dealing with other banks, and since that time its loans to individuals do not seem to have assumed very much general importance. By no means all of the banks have entered into direct relations with the central institution. The more important of the other banks have established close relationship with some of the smaller banks, but a considerable number of the latter seem to stand entirely alone with no means of securing assistance in emergencies.[21]

One common feature that the Bank of Japan shared with the National Bank of Belgium was that the amount of bankers' deposits held at the Bank was "insignificant."[22] Accordingly, "Any unusual demand for cash, however small, makes it necessary for the other banks to resort to it for loans."[23] Indeed, some of these advances "... have occasionally been made for rather long periods in connection with the rehabilitation of banking institutions which would otherwise have been forced into liquidation."[24]

The initial expansion of Japanese commercial banking stimulated the establishment of a vast number of small unit banks (2,355 banks in all in 1901 according to Sprague;[25] 1,867 in 1901 according to Patrick.[26] Given the small capital base, often illiquid assets, and loose relationships with larger banks, and thence the Central Bank, there were quite frequent runs on the small banks, notably in 1901 and 1907:[27]

> In handling emergencies the Bank of Japan does not take the immediate direction of affairs. Its staff is composed of officials rather than business men.... As has already been noted, the advances of the Bank are made principally to an extremely small number of borrowers. Probably the bulk of its business is with the comparatively small number of large banks, about forty in all, in Tokyo, Osaka, Kyoto, and Yokohama, whose business makes up about one-third that of all the banks. In coping with difficulties the lead is usually taken by representatives of some of these large banks and of the financial interests by which they are controlled.[28]

By 1910, "The effectiveness of the Bank of Japan as a resource in emergencies has been exhibited on a number of occasions."[29] So, virtually from its foundation, the Bank of Japan closely involved itself with the banking system, undertaking the micro functions of Central Banking.

Although the presence of the Central Bank did provide a central focus for the banking system,[30] there was, even so, perhaps less centralization than some of those in authority would have liked to see; "By establishing a Central Bank, it was expected that the evils of the financial system in vogue, which might be termed the feudal system, would be obviated, and it was also hoped that by converting the national banks into agencies or branches of the central banking institution, having a complete system of communication, an even operation would be attained, and the working of the entire machinery facilitated throughout the whole Empire."[31]

This latter did not happen. The note-issuing privilege, and the reserves held behind the notes, of the national banks were progressively transferred to the Bank of Japan by the law of 1883;[32] it was announced that the charters of the national banks, falling due between 1896 and 1899, would not be renewed, but on the termination of their charters they were allowed to, and mainly did, become ordinary banks,[33] and were not forced to become branches of the Bank of Japan.

Indeed, the Bank of Japan had only established nine branches by 1910 in the main domestic commercial centers, excluding Yokohama and Kobe, since foreign business was handled by the Yokohama Specie Bank.[34] "There has been no attempt by its means to furnish the people generally with banking facilities."[35] Nor did the Bank make much attempt to develop improved payments and transfer facilities throughout Japan: this was left to the private banks. Accordingly, the marked regional disparities in interest rates remained a feature in Japan during these years.[36] Sprague gives a partial excuse for the failure to attempt such functions on the grounds that the "... Bank does not seem to be properly equipped for such a task. It has less than 40 officials above the rank of clerk."[37]

Besides this (unattempted) function of equalizing interest rates over the country, it had been hoped that the establishment of the Bank would serve to lower the average rate of interest, which had been generally very high—often over 10%. "The rate of interest was ever on the increase, due to the withdrawal of capital from circulation and the fact that the banks were advancing large sums on long-term loans. But, with a Central Bank exclusively engaged in discounting bills and in making advances for short periods on the best bills, capital would be active and interest low. Such an institution would, in fact, regulate the rate of discount and largely that of interest."[38]

An important contributing reason for the high interest rates in

Japan was felt to be the drain of specie to pay for the deficit on foreign trade:

> There are times when European countries have a like experience, and the reason why, in those countries, the deficiency of specie is not severely felt, even under an unfavorable balance, may be found in the fact that there exists a financial institution for importing specie from abroad. Japan, in those days, had no such institution. There was an exit for specie, but no inlet for it; in other words, foreign goods were paid for in Japanese specie alone, and no other means were available for making the payment. It was realized that the establishment of Central Bank would open the way for bringing in foreign money.[39]

In the early years of its operations, from 1882[40] to 1914, the Bank, working together with the government and the Yokohama Specie Bank, was markedly successful in putting the external finance of Japan onto a sound basis, but much less successful in lowering the average rate of interest. Specie payments, convertibility, were resumed by the government in 1888; the whole note issue of the country was concentrated in the Bank of Japan shortly thereafter; Japan joined the Gold Standard in 1897. After an initial application to the Bank of Japan for funds to finance the Russo-Japanese War, the government was able to finance itself primarily with foreign loans, which left the Bank of Japan, after the end of the war, with greatly enhanced foreign exchange reserves.[41]

On the other hand, despite maintaining the external finance of Japan on a strong basis, the Bank made less of an obvious impact on the *general* level of domestic interest rates. Nevertheless,

> ... it is certain that the presence of the Bank has diminished the tendency of rates to advance to extremely high levels in periods of seasonal or extraordinary strain. This is in itself a very great gain. Indeed, it is evidence of the successful performance by a central bank of its primary function on the banking side. It is also possible that the operations of the Bank of Japan, by diminishing for other banks the risks arising out of general causes to which the business is subject, may have fostered the investment of capital in banking.

An examination of the actual course of rates for loans does not enable one to determine the effect upon them of the single influence of the Bank of Japan.... Rates for loans reached about as high levels in 1898 as in 1882 before the establishment of the Bank and were not much less at any time during the first fifteen years of its history than they were in 1883.... Rates are still high in Japan judged by western standards. In 1909 a discount rate of 4 per cent was for the first time quoted in Tokyo. The rates of the Bank of Japan have never been less than 5.8 per cent, and during the last ten years the maximum discount rate has been between 8.8 per cent and 6.2 per cent.[42]

Moreover, in the earlier years, prior to around 1900, the loans of the Bank of Japan were primarily made to other banks at below market rates: it was only from about 1903 onward that market rates were normally in line with, or below, that of the Bank.[43]

There are two interpretations of the continuing high level of Japanese interest rates. The first is that the Bank of Japan was initially constrained before 1905 by the need to maintain external convertibility, and from 1905–1907 by a wish to restrain a speculative boom, from extending larger loans and advances, and that, subject to such constraints, the Bank extended assistance as liberally as it could.[44] This view is shared by Patrick:

Although the central bank and the government at times in the next forty years [after 1888] allowed the discipline of the specie standard to manifest itself in reducing the money supply, when it came to the choice between severe depression or fiduciary money issue, the latter, more elastic route was usually taken. This is well indicated by the preliminary estimates of the growth of the money supply.... The generally expansive government fiscal policy, abetted by the Bank of Japan's active accommodation of both the government and the commercial banks, meant that the inflationary tendencies of the early years continued over the long run as well.[45]

A problem with this latter position is that the domestic assets, the loans, of the Bank of Japan remained so low during these years. A second interpretation, which Sprague appears to share, is that, beyond its external financial responsibilities (maintaining convertibility) and its micro function of supporting the banking system, the Bank of Japan had, in these years, a somewhat minimalist view of its macro-function role for influencing the general level of domestic interest rates and financial developments. Thus: "The amount which the Bank itself contributes to the available supply of credit in the country certainly does not seem to be so much as was expected when its establishment was proposed. The management of the Bank apparently regard it primarily as an organ for regulating the currency, for handling the financial business of the Government, and as a resource in emergencies rather than an instrument for directly assisting in the development of business activities."[46]

This minimalist view of its domestic macro-function responsibilities would be consistent with its inactive role in opening branches, facilitating payment transmission, equalizing regional interest rates, etc. Sprague was even concerned whether the Bank held a sufficiently large loan book to be able to make its rate effective, when it wanted to tighten markets, by reducing its domestic asset holdings.[47]

As in several other countries, those from Japan responding to the enquiries of the National Monetary Commission described their existing banking system in glowing terms, in each case sans pareil. Thus: "The banking system of Japan may be considered perfect at present and adequate to meet the prevailing condition of this country, and the efficiency of the Bank of Japan as the center of the banks of the whole country is very marked."[48] Hyperbole no doubt, but the development of the Japanese banking system as a whole from 1876 until 1914 was most impressive. This owed a great deal to the ability of the authorities to stabilize the currency and maintain external convertibility and improve the external finances of Japan, and notably to the Bank of Japan for its continued support for the commercial banks. If the Bank was, at the same time, somewhat slow to expand its domestic assets, this could be ascribed to a very proper caution, and its relative inaction in opening branches, facilitating payments, and unifying financial conditions across Japan could be ascribed to a desire to deal first with essentials while operating with a small staff.

Notes

Chapter 1

1. As also, it would appear, do Timberlake (1978) and Cameron (1967).
2. Also see Timberlake (1984, p. 1) and Schwartz (1984).
3. Also see Hayek (1984) and Friedman (1984).
4. See, for example, Leijonhufvud (1983).
5. This general approach has been nicely surveyed and summarized by Jao (1983).
6. For example, "Federal Reserve Policy in the 1973–1975 Recession: A Case Study of Fed Behavior in a Quandary," chapter 3 in Wachtel (1982). Also see Lombra and Moran (1980).
7. On this subject, see F. W. Fetter (1965), especially chapter IX, "The Victory of the Bagehot Principle."

Chapter 2

1. For a forthright restatement of this claim, see Cameron (1967, p. 313). Also see White (1984b).
2. For an excellent survey of this literature, see Jao (1983).
3. See, for example, Timberlake (1978, pp. 222–223): "The creation of a Bank of the United States, or for that matter a Bank of England, was no more than governmental chartering of a commercial banking institution that would also act as a banker for the government. Such an institution was first a commercial bank and second a public bank, and that was all so far as it founders were concerned." Also see Cameron (1967) for an account of the early banking history of several European countries and White (1984b).
4. Hayek (1976a, p. 16).
5. Also see, for example, Hayek (1960, p. 520).
6. Hayek (1976a, p. 16).
7. Hayek (1978).
8. See Hayek (1978), section XVII, "Monetary Policy Neither Deservable Nor Possible" especially pp. 101–102, "The Abolition of Central Banks".
9. Among recent studies on the earlier nineteenth-century discussions on 'free banking," White (1984b) is outstanding.

10. Also see the contributions by Currie, Cowen, Furstenberg, Peaver, and Tideman in "Symposium on Hayek's 'Standard," *Economic Affairs* (June/July 1986), pp. 30–39.
11. For a possible historical example of such a situation, see the appendix, in the section on the Swedish Riksbank.
12. Also note Klein's claim (1974, p. 433) "....at a given alternative cost of holding different monies, high confidence monies will drive out low confidence monies."
13. Timberlake (1978) also asserts that this will happen (see pp. 208, 225).

Chapter 3

1. The argument in this chapter depends heavily on the historical account of the free banking debates in the nineteenth century provided by Vera Smith, *The Rationale of Central Banking* (1936). A more recent and more comprehensive study of the debate in Britain, which became available to me only after I had started this work, is provided by White (1984b); also see Fetter (1965).

   I should, perhaps, also add that L. Pressnell wonders whether I have gone too far in suggesting that discussion of informational deficiencies did not play much of a role in these earlier debates. He cites (private correspondence) "... the 1844 Joint Stock Banking Code, which proved too strict to encourage formation of new, or transformation of existing, banks, provided for safety through information and accountability."
2. There are echoes of this earlier argument in Hayek (1978), which argues (pp. 52–53) that any attempt by a competitive bank to overissue would be, automatically, checked by a flight from that bank's currency.
3. The relationship between the Prussian Bank and the private banks in Prussia in the mid-nineteenth century provides an example; see Tilly (1967).
4. A similar example of such centripetal forces, at the international level, is to be found in the establishment and role of the Bank for International Settlements (BIS).
5. Also see Timberlake (1978, p. 190).
6. See Dorrance (1952).
7. Wilson (1952b).
8. Simkin (1952).
9. Wilson (1952a).
10. Duncan (1952).
11. Wilson (1952c).
12. Ibid., pp. 51, 63.
13. Ibid., p. 81.
14. Ibid., p. 86.
15. See *Interviews* on the banking and currency systems, National Monetary Commission (1901), Germany, with directors of the Dresdner Bank (pp. 416, 485–489).

16. Another example is provided by the foundation of the Société Centrale des Banques de Province in the 1890s by the small, unit local banks in France, which were under increasing competition from the Crédit institutions—see Liesse (1911, pp. 216–219).

17. Also, see Timberlake (1978, pp. 212–213) and Richard Sylla (1982, p. 31).

18. While the London clearing banks held interbank balances at the Bank of England, most smaller, unit country banks found it more convenient in the nineteenth century to hold correspondent balances with a London clearing bank rather than the Bank of England. There were, however, obvious problems, and potential conflicts of interest, in holding such deposits with one of the large branch banks that could well be, or become, a local competitor. So an increasing proportion of such interbank deposits went to a conservatively run London bank without a major branch network, Glyn Mills & Company.

19. *Money Trust Investigation*, testimony of W. Frew, December 10, 1912, pp. 631–634.

20. See, among others, Sprague (1910, 251–253), Noyes (1909, pp. 366–370), and Prussing (1907, pp. 426–471).

21. There appears to be at least one exception to this dictum. Olga Crisp, "Russia: 1860–1914," chapter VII in Cameron (1967), reports (p. 236) that, despite acting as a commercial bank and competitor with private banks, the relationship between the Russian State Bank and the commercial banks was excellent: "Both the public and the business community apparently found its [The State Bank's] moral position beyond reproach."

22. Also see Fetter (1965), especially chapter IX, "The Victory of the Bagehot Principle."

Chapter 4

1. The contrary arguments recently put forward by White (1984b, pp. 93–97) should also be considered.

2. Matthews (1954), chapter XI, "Money and Banking," describes in section 2, "The Bank of England and the Palmer Ruler" (pp. 165–175), how the Bank behaved at this time. Also see Fetter (1965).

3. An extreme example is provided by the Italian experience in 1885–1893—see the appendix.

4. Cameron (1967) claims (chapter 2, "Scotland, 1750–1845," and conclusion, p. 293) that the absence of restriction on entry into banking in Scotland provided "... a degree of competition not to be found in any other country." Unless the extent of competition is to be itself measured by the freedom of entry, it is not clear on what evidence this claim is based. Thus on p. 70, Cameron (1967) reports the collusive agreements of the two main Edinburgh banks in the eighteenth century, the Bank of Scotland and the Royal Bank. Although there were "18 note-issuing institutions at the beginning of the nineteenth century," Cameron notes that "typically a bank would have three or four branches,

usually in near-by satellite communities" plus often a branch in Glasgow, and the distribution of such note-issuing banks between centers, as noted by Cameron (p. 71), suggests local oligopolies in each major center (except perhaps Glasgow). Also see Checkland (1975), especially pp. 272–273.

5. On this, see Viner (1924) and Johnson (1910).

Chapter 5

1. For a rigorous analytical demonstration that, under conditions of perfect information, profit maximization will lead banks to choose strategies with zero probability of bankruptcy, see Kareken and Wallace (1978), especially p. 425.
2. See Hirsch (1977, pp. 241–243).
3. For a further early reference, and subsequent discussion, of this issue, see Kareken (1983).
4. Marais (1979).
5. See Federal Deposit Insurance Corporation, (1983) and Kareken (1983).
6. Besides these analysts, certain bodies, such as IBCA, have recently been established to attempt to standardize published accounts and to interview the banks involved. There are also the credit-rating agencies in the United States. I am grateful to J. Revell for reminding me of these.
7. See Korobow, Stuhr, and Martin (1977), Sinkey (1977), and Goodman and Shaffer (1983, p. 23). On the other hand, note Benston's warning (referring back to an earlier paper by Flannery and Guttentag), in Benston (1983, p. 13), that "these [early-warning] systems have not been validated; hence, we do not know how well or even whether they are effective for predicting failure. In fact, the systems appear to be used primarily as a more efficient means for the examiners to look at and structure data for their reports."
8. Also see Pettway and Sinkey (1980) and Pettway (1980).
9. So long as the smaller banks, without an active market for their equity, publish sufficient operating and accounting data, these could be used, in theory by all depositors (and in practice by bank examiners and large depositors), to look for early-warning signs of difficulties; see Pettway and Sinkey (1980, p. 137).
10. For a particularly dramatic exposition of how narrow Stock Exchanges can be managed, see Cornwell (1983), especially chapters 6 and 7, for an account of Roberto Calvi's manipulations of share prices, notably of Banco Ambrosiano.
11. See Klein (1974, p. 434), for an analysis of "confidence-producing expenditures" by banks as investments in "branch name capital."
12. Sinkey (1977) states (p. 782 and footnote 4) that "the major causes of bank failures have been dishonest and/or inept bank managers."
13. See Benston (1983, p. 12).
14. For example, Fraser and McCormack (1978) report that the risk premium on new issues of debt by banks rose only *after* the shock of the Franklin National Bank had occurred. "In this instance, however, there is no evidence of market response in anticipation of the Franklin failure" (footnote 3, p. 529).

15. See Moran (1984), especially chapter 1, section 3, "The Politics of Complexity," and chapter 3, section 8, "The Decline of Esoteric Politics."
16. Sandler and Tschirhart (1980) note (p. 1491) that "if members are heterogenous, then the provision, toll, and membership decisions are more difficult to reach owing to the aggregation of diverse preferences."
17. The question of the composition of the directors of the Federal Reserve Banks and the Federal Reserve Board was a major issue in the debates leading up to the Federal Reserve Act of 1913.

Chapter 6

1. Also see Gardener (1978), especially pp. 44–45, and Revell (1976).
2. On this subject, see McMahon (1984, pp. 49–50) and Flannery (1982), plus many others.
3. Also see Kareken (1983) and McCarthy (1980, especially p. 596).
4. See Guttentag and Herring (1982a, pp. 103–104) and McCarthy (1980, especially pp. 580, 595).
5. See also the review of these books by Goodhart (1987b).

Chapter 7

1. Fama (1980).
2. Except insofar as the Central Bank has a direct concern for the smooth and trouble-free operation of the payment system itself, e.g., the working of the clearinghouses and the settlement systems, as contrasted with the institutions providing the transactions services.
3. As has Henry Wallich (1984), in addition to several other US economists.
4. See Flux (1911, p. 17).
5. It would, of course, be just as simple to keep the value of each unit constant but alter the number of units owned by each depositor as asset values change. I cannot see why that shift in presentation should affect people's behavior in any way.
6. This analysis stems from Tobin (1958, pp. 65–86).
7. Building societies are entering more actively into the provision of payment services now that the Building Societies Act (1986) has been passed into law. Payments will normally be on the basis of their nominally fixed-value convertible liabilities. The example above, however, envisages building societies, in certain circumstances, also being prepared to monetize assets with a varying market value.
8. Mutual funds seeking to attract depositors, in part on the grounds of an offer to provide payments' services, face a trade-off in this respect. Because of depositors' familiarity with fixed-nominal-value convertible deposits as a basis for the payment system, some mutual funds, to attract such depositors, have

given commitments to hold the value of their liabilities (normally) at such a fixed nominal value. But this opens them up to runs as soon as the publicly observable value of their assets falls toward or below the (temporarily) fixed value of their liabilities. This happened with the UK Provident Institute in April 1986. White (1984a, p. 707) and Mervyn Lewis, in personal discussion, have reported such behavior among mutual funds in the United States and Australia, respectively.

9. There would still have to be protection against fraud, but that is a common requirement, not particularly related to the provision of transaction services.

10. Something of a half way house between a monetary unit and a bank demand deposit would be an indexed demand deposit provided by either a bank or another intermediary. It might actually be slightly more difficult technically to organize payment services on the basis of these, rather than on mutual funds invested in marketable assets, since the latter are continuously revalued, while the former have partly unanticipated jumps on discrete occasions with the publication of the RPI/CPI price index to which the deposit was related. Again, payment might only be guaranteed up to some minimum real or nominal balance. Some way would also have to be found to allow continuous revaluing of the deposits through the month in line with the anticipated change in the forthcoming RPI. Still, these technical problems should be surmountable. Given that there are fiscal advantages to most tax brackets of depositors in holding indexed rather than nominal deposits, i.e., no capital gains tax on the inflation element in the indexed deposit, whereas income tax on the whole nominal interest on ordinary deposits is charged less the allowance given against bank charges, and that, in the United Kingdom, riskless short-term assets for such an intermediary to hold exist in the form of government indexed bonds, it is surprising that no intermediary has yet started to offer indexed banking with both liabilities and assets in indexed form. Perhaps the most likely reason, besides inertia and setup costs, is that intermediaries basically require a combination of riskier and higher yielding assets, together with safe assets, to hold against liabilities, all denominated in the same form. The disincentive for intermediaries in the United Kingdom from setting up as indexed bankers is an apparent absence of borrowers prepared to take loans in indexed form. Why that should be so is beyond the scope of this study.

11. For surveys of this latter issue, see White (1984a) and McCallum (1985).

12. See, in particular, Kaufman (1987) and the references therein, notably Benston et al. (1986), especially chapter 8; Kane (1985), especially chapter 4; and Federal Reserve Bank of Chicago (1986).

13. Of course, the risk of a run still depends in part on maturity transformation by the bank, with the duration of liabilities being generally shorter than that of assets. But even if there was no maturity transformation, a fall of asset values relative to the nominally fixed value of liabilities would make depositors unwilling to roll over or extend further funds to the bank, except on terms that made

such depositors preferred creditors relative to depositors with later maturities, a course that would be subject to legal constraint. So, the absence of maturity transformation would delay the development of a run but would not stop depositors from running when, and as, they could.

14. Earlier US historical experience examined by Aharony and Swary (1983, pp. 305– 322) points in the same direction.

15. An interesting question, suggested to me by Mervyn Lewis, is to what extent banks obtain useful information about borrowers' conditions from their complementary function of operating the present payments system. Insofar as banks do obtain information that is useful for credit assessment from the handling of payment flows, this would provide a stronger economic rationale for the present combination of banking functions. Research into, and analysis of, the customarily private and confidential question of informational relationships between banks and their borrowers needs to be developed further; we cannot say with any confidence now how far banks benefit in seeking to assess credit worthiness from their provision of payment services.

16. This argument has been advanced by economists such as Leland and Pyle (1977, pp. 371–87), Baron (1982, pp. 955–976), and Diamond, (1984, pp. 393–414).

17. At least this will be so until and unless a large borrower runs into prospective problems in meeting contractual repayment obligations. To a casual observer, banks seem to try to limit the informational costs of making the initial loans, e.g., by resorting to standardized grading procedures; once a sizable borrower runs into difficulties, the bank responds by greatly increasing its monitoring activities, becoming often very closely involved with that borrower's future actions.

18. This is not, as it happens, a purely hypothetical question. The Muslim prohibition on interest payments is causing Islamic countries to require their banks to issue Mushariqi loans, which do represent a form of equity share in the project being financed. Students of banking theory and practice might find it informative to give closer study to Islamic banking.

19. Much recent literature on banking and credit has assumed that the borrower's selection and management of projects may not be observed by any outside party, even the banker himself. See, for example, Stiglitz and Weiss (1981, pp. 393–410) and (1983, pp. 912–927).

20. Insofar as constraints, either external or self-imposed, exist that stop the receiver from calling in loans outstanding at failed banks, this source of potential loss to society would be lessened. Even so, at a minimum, the borrower would lose the ability to obtain additional loans from the failing bank and that ability could be crucial to survival in a cyclical depression.

21. This feature of banking, whereby calling of loans by failed banks causes economic disruption, has been recently noted and modeled by Diamond and Dybvig (1983, pp. 401–419) and Bernanke (1983, pp. 257–276).

Appendix

Introduction

1. The following volumes, published by the National Monetary Commission (Washington: Government Printing Office) relate to foreign (i.e., other than US) banking systems. Each was published in 1911, except for the first Senate Document noted below, which was published in 1910. The volumes sometimes contain several separate Senate Documents, bound together. The individual Senate Document numbers are separately recorded in brackets.

Vol. VIII   *The English Banking System*, comprising:
- "The English Banking System" by Hartley Withers, Sir R. H. Inglis Palgrave, and others (No. 492, 1910)
- "The Bank of England and Its Financial Services to the State" by E. von Philippovich and H. S. Foxwell (No. 591, 1911)

Vol. IX   *Banking in Canada*, comprising:
- "The History of Banking in Canada" by R. M. Breckenridge (No. 332)
- "The Canadian Banking System" by J. F. Johnson (No. 583)
- "Interviews on the Banking and Currency Systems of Canada" (No. 584)

Vol. X   *The Reichsbank and Renewal of Its Charter*, comprising:
- "The Reichsbank, 1876–1900" by the Reichsbank (No. 408)
- "Renewal of Reichsbank Charter"—additional material bearing on the renewal of the charter including discussions in the financial press by Dr. Koch, Prof. Lexis, Dr. Stroell, and others (No. 507)

Vol. XI   *Articles on German Banking and German Banking Laws*, comprising:
- "Miscellaneous Articles on German Banking" by Robert Franz, Waldemar Mueller, Dr. Carl Melchior, and others (No. 508)
- "German Imperial Banking Laws" by Dr. R. Koch (No. 574)

Vols. XII and XIII   *The German Bank Inquiry of 1908 (Stenographic Reports)*, Part 1 (Vol. XII) and Part 2 (Vol. XIII) (No. 407)

Vol. XIV   *The Great German Banks* by J. Riesser (No. 593)

Vol. XV   *Banking in France and the French Bourse*, comprising:
- "Evolution of Credit and Banks in France" by A. Liesse (No. 522)
- "The Bank of France in Its Relation to National and International Credit" by M. Patron (No. 494)
- "The History and Methods of the Paris Bourse" by E. Vidal (No. 573)

Vol. XVI   *Banking in Belgium and Mexico*, comprising:
- "The National Bank of Belgium" by C. A. Conant (No. 400)
- "The Banking System of Mexico" by C. A. Conant (No. 493)

Vol. XVII   *Banking in Sweden and Switzerland*, comprising:
- "The Swedish Banking System" by A. W. Flux (No. 576)
- "The Swiss Banking Law" by Dr. J. Landmann (No. 401)

Vol. XVIII   *Banking in Italy, Russia, Austro-Hungary and Japan*, comprising:

- "Italian Banks of Issue" by T. Canovai and D. F. Ferraris (No. 575)
- "Banking in Russia, Austro-Hungary, Holland and Japan" (No. 586), including
  a. "Organization of Banking in Russia" by Professors Idelson and Lexis
  b. "The Austro-Hungarian Bank" by R. Zuckerkandl
  c. "The Bank of the Netherlands" by R. van der Borght
  d. "The Banking System of Japan" by Marquis Katsura, Baron Sakatani, S Naruse, and O. M. W. Sprague

Vol. XIX   *Administrative Features of National Banking Laws and European Fiscal and Postal Savings Systems*, including
  a. "Fiscal Systems of England, France, Germany and the United States" by J. O. Manson (No. 403)
  b. "Notes on the Postal Savings-Bank Systems of the Leading Countries" (No. 658)

2. *Interviews on the Banking and Currency Systems of England, Scotland, France, Germany, Switzerland and Italy*, National Monetary Commission, Senate Document 405 (1910).

The Reichsbank

1. See, for example, *Renewal of Reichsbank Charter*, pp. 59–61.
2. See, for example, the article by W. Lexis, "Concerning the Renewal of the Reichsbank Privilege," from *Bank-Archive*, 1907, reproduced in *Renewal of Reichsbank Charter*, pp. 233–259.
3. Thus, in the interview with Herr Lottner, director of the Prussian State Bank (*Interviews on the Banking and Currency Systems*, 1910), he said (p. 365), "Frederick the Great founded the Seehandlung [another name for the Prussian State Bank] to promote Prussian trade, especially the over-sea trade," and, in answer to the question (p. 361), "What are the particular functions of the bank?" he replied, "In the first place it is an organization to help the State of Prussia. The principal part of the business is to finance the loans of the State...."
4. See the article by Dr. Koch, "Credit at the Reichsbank," reproduced in *Renewal of Reichsbank Charter*, pp. 203–215.
5. *Interviews*, p. 347.
6. Indeed (*The Reichsbank*, p. 37), "The Reichsbank did not hesitate to sustain losses through the tax [on excess notes beyond the contingent] when public interest required an extension of its note emission."
7. *Renewal of the Reichsbank Charter*, p. 238.
8. Ibid., pp. 245–259, especially pp. 248–249.
9. Also see the *Interview* with Herr Dr. von Glasenapp of the Reichsbank, pp. 346–347.
10. Paper by Dr. Stroell, *Renewal of Reichsbank Charter*, p. 246.
11. See the address by Dr. Damme at the Third German Bankers' Convention

(Hamburg, 1907), reproduced in *Renewal of Reichsbank Charter*, pp. 186–187, and also the article in the *Frankfurter Zeitung*, reporting on the German Bank Inquiry of 1908, reproduced in *Renewal of Reichsbank Charter*, p. 72.

12. See, again, the article in the *Frankfurter Zeitung*, reproduced in *Renewal of Reichsbank Charter*, p. 72, and *Interviews*, with Herr Mankiewitz and Herr Blinzig of the Deutsche Bank, p. 38.

13. *Interviews*, p. 375, with Herr Mankiewitz and Herr Blinzig of the Deutsche Bank: "It is not possible for us to say how much real money there is in the vaults of the banks, but we have so much money and gold in circulation and in the pockets of our people that there is no concern over the small cash holdings in the banks, as the public has the money in its pockets." Also see the discussion at the Third German Banks' Convention (Hamburg 1907) reproduced in *Renewal of Reichsbank Charter*, pp. 123–200.

14. Ibid., p. 165

15. See the address to the Third German Banks' Convention by Dr. Jaffe, reproduced in *Renewal of Reichsbank Charter*, pp. 125–143.

The Swiss National Bank

1. As also was the site of the Bank, with the merits of both Zurich, as the financial center, and Berne, the seat of the federal administration, being strongly supported. One round of parliamentary discussions on the formation of the Bank, in 1901, failed on this issue. In the end a compromise worthy of Solomon was adopted; the Bank was divided into two parts, with supervision and general management in Berne and business operations and the Direktorium in Zurich. See Dr. J. Landmann, "The Swiss Banking Law,' in *Banking in Sweden and Switzerland*, National Monetary Commission, Vol. XVIII (1911), pp. 109, 152–157, 170–176.

2. *Interviews*, Mr. Rueff, managing director of London branch of Swiss Bankverein, p. 502.

3. Ibid., p. 507; also see Dr. J. Landmann, op. cit., pp. 82–132.

4. Landmann, ibid, pp. 30–31.

5. Ibid., p. 11.

6. Ibid., p. 13.

7. Ibid., pp. 13–15.

8. Ibid., pp. 15–17.

9. Ibid., pp. 18, 24–27.

10. Ibid., p. 25.

11. *Interviews*, Mr. Rueff, p. 507.

12. The Act of 1881 required that "the balance sheets had to be periodically published under the supervision of the federal authorities. This control was vested in the Swiss fiscal department…, and a special board of inspectors for banks of issue was created" (Landmann, op. cit., p. 27).

13. *Interviews*, Mr. Rueff, p. 501; Landmann, op. cit., p. 26.

14. Landmann, ibid., p. 35.

15. Ibid., p. 42.
16. Ibid., pp. 45–47.
17. Ibid., pp. 83–85.
18. Ibid., p. 7.
19. Ibid., pp. 42–46.
20. Ibid., pp. 75–81.
21. There were some doubts about the cantonal guaranties that could be used in some cases instead of commercial bills.
22. Ibid., p. 55.
23. In part caused by those who would have lost by a transfer of the property rights of (taxing) seignorage from the cantons to the Confederation (ibid., pp. 99–100).
24. *Interviews*, Mr. Rueff, p. 507.
25. Ibid., p. 503. Restrictions on the permissible business of the Central Bank, in order to prevent competition, to delimit areas of responsibility, and to maintain the position of the existing banks, had been included at an early stage in the plans for the SNB, as reported in Landmann, op. cit., particuarly in his report of the theses presented by Hauser to the Nationalrat in 1893, pp. 94–96, and also 187–188.
26. Ibid., p. 505.

The Banque de France

1. Liesse (1911, pp. 16–17).
2. Liesse, ibid., p. 12, notes that "this bank was called 'caisse' for, as we have said, the word bank, recalling that of Law [Banque Générale], still terrified the public." Indeed, throughout the nineteenth century, banking institutions generally preferred to be described as credit institutions—e.g., Crédit Lyonnais.
3. Ibid., pp. 18–21.
4. Ibid., pp. 23–25.
5. Ibid., p. 22.
6. Ibid., pp. 32–33.
7. And also, because of the same distrust of bankers, specified that the regent's council should contain at least 5 (out of 15) businessmen.
8. Ibid., p. 33.
9. Ibid., p. 33.
10. Liesse, op. cit., p. 27.
11. Ibid., p. 33.
12. For example, it was firmly stated by M. Moret, manager of the Banque de Paris et des Pays-Bas, *Interviews*, p. 271, that it was not the aim of the Banque de France to maximize shareholders' profits. Also M. Pallain, the governor of the Banque de France, stated, *Interviews*, p. 217, that "the mission of the Bank ... is to moderate, as much as possible, the conditions of credit. The accomplishment of what it considers as its own particular task would appear to it incomparably

more desirable than the profits which it might obtain by measures such as those to which you allude."

13. Ibid., p. 141.

14. Ibid., p. 227.

15. Liesse, op. cit., pp. 149–150.

16. Note, for example, the requirements imposed on the Bank at the time of the renewal of its privilege in 1897, as described in Liesse, ibid., pp. 226–227; also the interview with M. Pallain, governor of the Bank of France, *Interviews*, pp. 202–203.

17. Ibid., pp. 89–90; "Finally, ten years after the law of 1857, the Bank could be compelled to establish branches in the departments where they did not exist. The Bank was in no hurry to found these branches. In 1867, although ten years after the law, 25 departments were still unprovided for."

18. Patron (1911, pp. 86–88).

19. This behavior is well documented—see, for example, Liesse, op. cit., pp. 45, 50–52, and Cameron, (1967, Chapter IV, "France," pp. 124–127, The Suppression of Competition").

20. Liesse, op. cit., pp. 72–75.

21. Ibid., p. 93.

22. Ibid., p. 65.

23. Patron, op. cit., pp. 75–76, records the accusation that the Bank was a "closed institution, accessible only to a few persons, to rich people and great industries, multiplying and complicating formalities, in order to keep the great public away...."

24. See the various interviews with French bankers in *Interviews and Patron*, op. cit., p. 73.

25. Liesse, op. cit., p. 196.

26. Ibid., pp. 73, 181.

27. op. cit., p. 27.

28. Ibid., p. 32.

29. Liesse, op. cit., p. 33.

30. Patron, op. cit., pp. 31–32.

31. Ibid., p. 86.

32. Ibid., p. 45.

33. Ibid., p. 87.

34. Ibid., pp. 56–57.

35. Ibid., pp. 127–128; also see Patron, op. cit., pp. 124, 127, 138.

36. Patron, ibid., pp. 125–127.

37. Ibid., p. 129.

38. Ibid., p. 137.

39. Liesse, op. cit., p. 115; "At bottom this measure favoured the Bank of France."

40. Liesse, ibid., pp. 196–197, 181.

41. To be contrasted with the Banque de Paris et des Pays-Bas, which was more of an investment bank, financing itself more by capital than through deposits,

and dealing largely in company securities: see *Interviews* with M. Moret, its manager, p. 268; and also from the specialist financial intermediaries, the Crédit Foncier and Crédit Agricole, see Liesse, op. cit., pp. 241–267 and *Interviews*, pp. 277–291, 309–323.

42. Patron, op. cit., pp. 75–76.
43. Op. cit., p. 200.
44. The local, and provincial, banks, however, suffered from the combined competition of the Banque de France and the credit companies—see Liesse, ibid., pp. 164, 217–223. They reacted by trying to form a union, and founded, in 1905, a bank in Paris to provide them with quasi-Central Banking facilities, the Société Centrale des Banques de Province.
45. *Interviews*, with Baron Brincard of the Crédit Lyonnais, p. 239:

> Q. Do you find that the Bank of France competes with you in any way?
> A. In no way.

Also see interview with M. Ullmann of the Comptoir d'Escompte, ibid., p. 264.
46. Op. cit., p. 176.
47. Patron, op. cit., pp. 46–47.
48. Liesse, op. cit., pp. 184–185.
49. Ibid., pp. 190–191.
50. Ibid., p. 191.
51. Patron, op. cit., p. 157, notes that the Bank manages credit "without trammeling the freedom of action of other banks. It confines itself to serving them as regulator, and intervenes only so far as is necessary to curb speculation, and thus to protect credit against all dangers."
52. *Interviews*, with Baron Brincard of the Crédit Lyonnais, p. 241;

> Q. Are you examined at any time and in any way by the Government?
> A. No. The control of the Government is limited to the supervision for taxes....

Also with M. Ullmann of the Comptoir d'Escompte, p. 261:

> Q. There is no government supervision of your bank?
> A. No.

53. Liesse, op. cit., pp. 150–160.
54. Patron, op. cit., pp. 12–14.
55. This preference was reinforced by general adherence to the real bills doctrine. Thus in the interview with M. Pallain, governor of the Banque de France, *Interviews*, p. 213, he was asked,

> Q. The fluctuations are more or less automatic? If there is an excess of notes, it is, I assume, soon taken care of by presentation for redemption.
> A. The mechanism is quite automatic. When circumstances demand a reduction of issue the notes are naturally presented for redemption, and it

seems to us that as long as this redemption is made without difficulty, there can never be an excess of notes in circulation.

Also see ibid., pp. 211, 212, and Patron, op. cit., pp. 27–32.
56. Ibid., pp. 140–146.

The Swedish Riksbank

1. The occasion of its downfall is unusual in banking history. It took in copper coin, then the metallic currency of Sweden, against receipts, credit notes, which became used as currency. Naturally it began to extend loans, so that the volume of its note issue soon much exceeded its copper coin reserve. At that juncture, there was a *rise* in the market price of copper. Depositors sought to withdraw the metal by presenting the notes, and the bank ran into difficulties. This, and all other information in this section on the Riksbank, is taken from Flux (1911)—in this case, pp. 14–15.

2. Ibid., p. 16.

3. Ibid., p. 101; also see pp. 16–17.

4. There were various attempts to set up discount banks, usually in conjunction with the Riksbank, which would have private shareholders. These banks would use funds from capital, advances from and rediscounts to the Riksbank, and deposits (but not note issue, though in some cases their drafts did serve as a circulating medium) to discount commercial paper—ibid., pp. 21–27. These private discount banks generally ran into trouble, often through excessive, rash, and illiquid loans. Following the collapse of the Malmo business in 1817, both the Gothenburg institutions were also compelled to liquidate, and "Private credit institutions could no longer command sufficient public confidence, and the Parliament resolved that the Riksbank's discount agency ... should alone be permitted to conduct the business of discounting throughout the Kingdom. One result was the establishment in 1824 of branches of the Riksbank in Gothenburg and Malmo" (ibid., p. 27).

5. In 1789, when the national finances were in difficulties, owing to war and mismanagement, the control of the public debt was transferred to Parliament. A national debt office was set up "... which created a new circulating medium in the shape of certificates bearing interest at 3 per cent, and of small face value."

Klein (1974) argues that interest-bearing and non-interest-bearing currencies can coexist side by side, if the former is depreciating relative to the latter just enough to offset the interest payment. It is interesting that by 1790 "... a premium of 6 per cent was established on bank notes in terms of debt certificates" (ibid., p. 23). Nevertheless, this situation was not felt to be a "metastable equilibrium," to use Klein's phrase. Parliament made the certificates a forced currency and dropped the interest payment. Even so, and despite issuing smaller denominations, which were generally easier to keep in circulation, the debt certificates continued to depreciate against the bank's notes (ibid., p. 23). An interesting case study, perhaps, for the new school of monetary theorists?

6. Again unusually, the bank "... when it passed under the control of the Parliament, had been expressly denied the right to issue credit notes to circulate as currency" (ibid., p. 18). However, the bank soon came to provide transfer notes in the form of deposit receipts, and such was the need for a paper currency as a circulating medium that they became used as such: "It was not till 1836 that the notes of the bank were drawn in the form of a promissory note instead of that of a deposit receipt" (ibid., p. 19).

7. Under the law of 1886, "They were expressly forbidden to issue anything of the nature of bank notes. Their deposit receipts were required to be expressly transferable only by endorsement, and to bear the statement that they were not for use as a circulating medium" (ibid., p. 106).

8. Indeed, the earlier act of 1846 had appointed government inspectors to take part in marking up each bank's quarterly report, which had to be rendered to the crown (ibid., p. 36).

9. This harked back to the earliest days of the bank, which was organized on the basis of two supposedly separate departments, the loan department financing loans on the basis of deposits and the issue department supplying credit notes on the receipt of coin and specie. Even when Palmstruch's private bank had been taken over by Parliament, "A secret instruction, however, authorized the advance by the exchange department to the lending department of the funds at its disposal though on reasonably moderate terms" (ibid., p. 17). Thus, as early as 1668, the pursuit of a 100% reserve ratio collapsed in the face of commercial pressures.

10. In the crisis of 1857, when the ability of the bank to provide assistance by rediscounting domestic bills was constrained, "An association was formed among certain members of the exchange for mutual assistance, and they presented for discount to the Riksbank bills for large amounts drawn on a Swedish merchant who paid a visit to Hamburg" (ibid., pp. 81–82).

11. Ibid., pp. 128–129: "It has been alleged that the other banks found a difficulty in securing the help they needed from the Riksbank. The monthly accounts hardly lend support to this view. It is doubtless true that, at a time of pressure, the rules requiring careful scrutiny of bills offered for discount at the Riksbank were more scrupulously observed than at ordinary times. But the figures ... show that it provided in substantially increased sums the funds called for by those who depended on it, and this means the other banks in the main."

The Danish National Bank

1. Although the government relinquished ownership of the bank, it maintained representation on the managing body, with first one and subsequently two appointees on the five man governing directorate.

Banca d'Italia

1. C. F. Ferraris, "The Italian Banks of Issue," from *Banking in Italy, Russia, Austro-Hungary and Japan,* National Monetary Commission, Vol. XVIII (1911), p. 207.

2. T. Canovai, "The Banks of Issue in Italy," from *Banking in Italy, Russia, Austro-Hungary and Japan,* National Monetary Commission, Vol. XVIII (1911), p. 18.

3. Ibid., p. 26.

4. Canovai, *European Interviews,* National Monetary Commission, Vol. I (1910), p. 516.

5. In 1879 their notes in circulation were as follows, in millions of lire (from Canovai, "The Banks of Issue in Italy," op. cit., p. 47):

Banca Nazionale	441
Banca Nazionale Toscana	59
Banca Toscana di Credito	14
Banca Romana	44
Banco di Napoli	145
Banco di Sicilia	30

6. Ibid., p. 29.

7. Ibid., p. 33.

8. Ibid., p. 41.

9. Ibid., p. 48.

10. Ibid., pp. 54–55.

11. See chapter IV, "The Crédit Foncier or Realty Credits of the Banca Nazionale nel Regno D'Italia," ibid., pp. 62–70.

12. Ibid., p. 21.

13. Ibid., p. 22.

14. Ferraris, op. cit., p. 221. Whereas the Church has evinced some pastoral antipathy to the works of bankers, moneylenders, usurers, etc., equally it is the case that the forays of the Church itself into the banking world have not excited the admiration of bankers.

15. See Canovai, chapter 5, "Excess of Building at Rome."

16. Ibid., pp. 77, 83.

17. Ibid., p. 108.

18. Not many economists can have precipitated such a massive, though long overdue, crisis. Canovai approved of his action and described him as "the illustrious economist who is an honor to Italy" (ibid., p. 109). He generally thought well of economists, describing another, Ferrara, as "the glory of economic science" (ibid., p. 85). He was not so well inclined toward politicians, describing their reaction to Pantaleoni's revelation, as follows: "The politicians, who had suddenly scented, in the sad rottenness of the Banca Romana, a most excellent excuse for giving free play to the cannibal instinct that distinguishes them from the rest of the human race" (ibid., p. 111). Canovai's prose is occasionally purple, but his heart was in the right place!

19. The size ratio was as follows (ibid., pp. 125, 151):

Banca d'Italia	30
Banco di Napoli	4
Banco di Sicilia	2

20. *European Interviews*, p. 519.
21. Under the law of 1893, note holders had the right of redemption in specie, but that law initially could not be enforced since it would have led to an unacceptable reserve drain. Instead, the legal tender, irredeemable nature of the notes was rolled forward from year to year. Improved economic conditions allowed the exchange rate with France to return to par in 1902, and to remain there until the war, but even so, the status of the notes was reaffirmed each year after 1902 as legal tender. On this see Canovai, *European Interviews*, pp. 513, 524, and Ferraris, op. cit., pp. 224–225.
22. Ferraris, ibid., pp. 222–223, 234, and Canovai, "The Banks of Issue in Italy," pp. 150, 157–158.
23. Ferraris, op. cit., p. 226.
24. Canovai, op. cit., p. 142.
25. Ferraris, op. cit., pp. 250–251, and Canovai, op. cit., p. 127.
26. Ferraris, op. cit., pp. 234–242, and Canovai, op. cit., pp. 120–123.
27. Canovai, "The Banks of Issue in Italy," p. 145; Ferraris, "The Italian Banks of Issue," p. 247; Canovai, *European Interviews*, p. 523.
28. Ferraris, op. cit., p. 248, and Canovai, *European Interviews*, p. 523.
29. Canovai, "The Banks of Issue in Italy," p. 146.
30. Canovai, op. cit., pp. 171–204.
31. Canovai, ibid., p. 184, provides a balance sheet for the three banks of issue (millions of lire):

	Dec. 31, 1984	Dec. 31, 1908
Assets gold	433	1,179
Silver	80	132
Liabilities notes	1,126	1,862
Demand deposits	325	343
Reserve ratio (%)	42	74

32. Ibid., p. 163.
33. Ferraris, op. cit., pp. 244–246.
34. Canovai, *European Interviews*, p. 537.
35. Ibid., pp. 511, 537–540.
36. Ibid., pp. 526–527.
37. Canovai, "The Banks of Issue in Italy," pp. 81–84.
38. Ibid., pp. 90–93.
39. Ibid., pp. 133–134.
40. Canovai, *European Interviews*, p. 538, and "The Banks of Issue in Italy," p. 174.
41. Ibid., p. 175.

The Austro-Hungarian Bank

1. Zuckerkandl, "The Austro-Hungarian Bank," in *Banking in Italy, Russia, Austro-Hungary and Japan*, National Monetary Commission, Vol. XVIII (1911), p. 116, "Statistical Tables."
2. Ibid., pp. 57–63.
3. Ibid., p. 60.
4. Ibid., p. 70.
5. Ibid., p. 71.
6. Ibid., p. 65.
7. Ibid., p. 65. It was indeed the imperial commissary who was most concerned about the dangers of disclosure of the Bank's true affairs (ibid., p. 72).
8. Ibid., p. 65.
9. Ibid., p. 72.
10. Ibid., p. 73.
11. Ibid., pp. 76–83.
12. Ibid., p. 92.
13. Ibid., pp. 92–94.
14. Ibid., p. 90.
15. Ibid., pp. 89–90.
16. Ibid., pp. 95–96.
17. Ibid., pp. 98–99.
18. Ibid., p. 102.
19. Ibid., p. 110.
20. Ibid., p. 110.
21. Also ibid., p. 113.
22. Ibid., p. 108.
23. Ibid., p. 100.
24. See the reported quotation from a lecture by Professor von Bilinski, the governor (1906) of the Austro-Hungarian Bank (ibid., pp. 112–113).
25. Ibid., p. 106.
26. Ibid., p. 111.
27. Ibid., p. 105.
28. Ibid., p. 83.
29. Ibid., p. 84.
30. Ibid., pp. 83–84.
31. Ibid., p. 104.
32. Ibid., p. 106. Its giro business grew from 1,634 mn crowns in 1887 to 63,626 mn crowns in 1907 (ibid., p. 118).
33. Ibid., p. 116.

The National Bank of Belgium

1. Conant (1911, p. 12).
2. Ibid., p. 5.
3. Ibid., p. 13.

4. Ibid., p. 14.
5. Ibid., p. 14.
6. Ibid., p. 14.
7. On this, see Cameron (1967) chapter V, "Belgium, 1800–1875," pp. 129–150.
8. Conant (1911, p. 15).
9. Ibid., p. 16.
10. Ibid., p. 88.
11. Ibid., pp. 85–89.
12. Ibid., pp. 37–44.
13. Ibid., p. 6.
14. Ibid., p. 180. Conant does not, however, record any instance of the authorities feeling the need to exercise this option.
15. The Bank was, however, obliged to invest any surplus above the government's operational requirements in commercial paper (ibid., pp. 156–157).
16. Ibid., p. 194.
17. Ibid., p. 94.
18. Conant records in some detail the "luminous argument" on this subject made by M. Pirmez in 1872 on the occasion of the revision of the Bank's charter. Indeed, students of the history of the debate on the proper definition of money could still read these pages (ibid., pp. 93–95) with advantage.
19. Ibid., p. 89.
20. Formally the Bank had only one branch, in Antwerp, but also had a network of agencies, most of which (30) were associated with a local discount office (ibid., pp. 115–120). The government required the Bank to open agencies in some cases, despite lack of commercial business, in centers where public transactions needed to be undertaken. The agents were also, like the governor, appointed by the king (ibid., p. 118).
21. Ibid., pp. 65–67.
22. Ibid., p. 193.
23. Ibid., p. 31.
24. Ibid., pp. 157–163. This was also conservatively run: "It aimed not merely to implant the principle of economy, but sought to surround the withdrawal of deposits with such formalities and disadvantages as would deter depositors from making unwise use of their savings after they had been accumulated" (ibid., p. 158).
25. Ibid., p. 159.
26. Ibid., p. 34.
27. Ibid., pp. 19–22. Prior to 1872, the Bank was only *legally* required to redeem its notes in specie at its head office in Brussels; after 1872, the obligation was also extended to the agencies, subject to notice. The Bank's notes, though receivable in public dues from the outset, were only made legal tender in 1873, but only so long "... as they continued to be redeemed in legal coin" (ibid., pp. 73–74).
28. Ibid., p. 79.

29. Ibid., p. 7.
30. Ibid., p. 104.
31. Ibid., p. 102.
32. Ibid., p. 7.
33. Ibid., p. 60: "The National Bank of Belgium has followed a policy in fixing the rate of discount which has conformed in a measure to the English policy of changing the rate with changes in condition, but has leaned in some degree toward the French policy of keeping the rate uniform, except under the pressure of great necessity."
34. Ibid., p. 9. One of the reasons for reducing the level of discount rate, at which all excess earnings accrued to the government, not the Bank, was to ensure that "... when the discount rate was raised to an abnormal figure ... the action of the Bank should be free from suspicion." It was also thought to reinforce "... the firm determination of the Bank to do all which lay in its power to maintain discount at favorable rates while it was practicable, even at the price of considerable sacrifices." The latter is a quotation from Senator Descamps on the occasion of the change to a lower level for the tax on excess earnings in 1900 (ibid., p. 137).
35. Ibid., p. 190.
36. Despite certain (rather feeble) direct attempts to constrain the export of silver coin, "The railway officials have taken steps to prevent important transfers of silver in the form of ordinary baggage, and ticket sellers and treasury officials have been forbidden to make exchanges of money except within the normal limits" (ibid., p. 202).
37. Ibid., pp. 163–192, 201–202.

The Bank of Japan

1. On the advice of Assistant Secretary of Finance Ito (later Prince Ito), who "... was sent to the United States to study our banking and financial arrangements. After a brief examination he reported in favor of the establishment in Japan of a banking system modeled upon that of this country"—in O.M.W. Sprague, "The Banking System of Japan," section IV of *Banking in Italy, Russia, Austro-Hungary and Japan*, National Monetary Commission, Vol. XVIII (1911), p. 179.
2. H. T. Patrick, "Japan: 1868–1914," chapter VIII of *Banking in the Early Stages of Industrialization*, in Cameron (1976), p. 249.
3. Baron Sakatani (ex-minister of finance), "Opinions: The Banking System of Japan," section II, op. cit., p. 141. The papers to the National Monetary Commission entitled "The Banking System of Japan" are unique in that they include a contribution from the then prime minister and minister of finance, Marquis Katsura, section I; an ex-minister of finance, Baron Sakatani, section II; a Japanese financier, Mr. S. Naruse, section III; and an (eminent) US monetary economist, O. M. W. Sprague.
4. "The Banking System of Japan," section I, p. 121.
5. Op. cit., p. 245.

6. The latter were "... engaged in the multiple functions of trade, and even production, as well as finance" (ibid., p. 246).

7. On this latter matter, see Patrick, ibid., pp. 256–257; otherwise, for an account of the first national bank experiment, see "The Banking System of Japan," passim.

8. S. Naruse, "Opinions, The Banking System of Japan," section III, p. 151, but also see other sections.

9. Sprague, op. cit., p. 183.

10. Ibid., p. 184.

11. Patrick, op. cit., p. 267.

12. Baron Sakatani, "Opinions: The Banking System of Japan," section II, op. cit., p. 144. There were, however, certain differences of view on the relative priority that might be placed on the achievement of external financial objectives, as compared with domestic monetary stabilization. Thus Kinzo Shima, in private correspondence, has translated a section on this topic from the recent publication (in Japanese) *A Hundred Years' History of the Bank of Japan* as follows:

> Minister of Finance, Matsukata, found it necessary to introduce a new system under which the Yokohama Specie Bank could enjoy central bank credit preferentially and permanently in the financing of foreign trade in order to increase specie reserves, which was one of the most important subjects at that time, by stimulating exports.
>
> On the other hand, the Governor of the Bank of Japan, Tomita, laid stress on the fundamentals of monetary policy from the central bank's position, by insisting that the central bank, whose responsibility was the maintenance of the conversion system and stabilization of the value of currencies, could not admit any preferential treatment which might make its monetary control difficult, even if it would contribute to a certain purpose.

This dispute ended in the government's victory, and the establishment of the special relationship between the Yokohama Specie Bank and the Bank of Japan, as stated. Nevertheless, given the Bank of Japan's own concerns and objectives, the extent of cooperation between the two banks is, perhaps, more debatable than suggested by Sakatani.

13. "The Banking System of Japan," section I, op. cit., p. 126.

14. Sprague, op. cit., p. 186. Certainly the two Central Bank Acts, of Belgium and Japan, were similar. One of the attractions of the statutory basis of the National Bank of Belgium in the eyes of the Japanese may have been that the government's legal authority as a supervisor of the National Bank of Belgium was stronger than in the case of the Bank of England or the Banque de France. Thus in *A Hundred Years' History of the Bank of Japan*, it was stated that "what Minister of Finance, Matsukata, did learn through the investigation of the Belgian experience was not how to limit the government control over the central bank but how to ensure it effectively."

15. Prime Minister Katsura, op. cit., p. 132.
16. Baron Sakatani, op. cit., p. 142. On the other hand, it is possible to envisage that the share ownership by the imperial household in the Bank of Japan may have enhanced the latter's desire for profits. Also, it has been said that the Bank of Japan was concerned with prospective income and expenditure flows when deciding whether to establish a new branch.
17. Naruse, op. cit., p. 159; also see p. 166, in which he argues that, in return for the note-issuing privilege, "... the Government must control the selection of bills, bonds, etc., to be received, directing the business of the Bank and controlling the nomination of its staff."
18. Sprague, op. cit., p. 211.
19. Patrick, op. cit., p. 252.
20. Naruse, op. cit., p. 160. He continues that "the unavoidable result of this was that some banks, taking advantage of this situation, made it their chief business to earn the amount of the difference for themselves by becoming intermediaries between private individuals and the Bank of Japan." Also see p. 173, where he states that "the Bank of Japan keeps the [interest] rate at a low point at all times, and makes it her constant object to prop up the ordinary banks." On this also see Sprague, op. cit., p. 186.
21. Sprague, op. cit., p. 192.
22. Sprague, op. cit., p. 201. The liabilities of the Bank consisted primarily of notes and of government deposits; by comparison, other deposits were extremely small—see the table produced by Sprague (ibid., p. 190). During these same years, however, the deposits of commercial banks were growing rapidly—see Patrick, op. cit., table VIII.3, p. 264. Clearly the Bank did not seek to compete with commercial banks for ordinary deposits, and so was noncompetitive, but there is no discussion of that. Perhaps by 1882 it was regarded as the obvious course for a newly established Central Bank.
23. Sprague, op. cit., p. 201.
24. Ibid., p. 197.
25. Ibid., p. 188.
26. Op. cit., p. 265. Subsequent research puts the number of banks in 1901 as follows:

Specialized banks	5
Agriculture and industry banks	46
Ordinary banks	1,890
Savings banks	444
	2,385

Therefore, the number according to Sprague (2,355 banks) corresponds to the total, and the number according to Patrick (1,867) to the ordinary banks, respectively, with some error. The number of banks in 1901 was, however, the peak in Japanese banking history.
27. Patrick, op. cit., p. 265. Also Sprague, op. cit., pp. 204–208.

28. Sprague, ibid., p. 207.

29. Ibid., p. 206.

30. Baron Sakatani, op. cit., p. 144: "The entire banking system of Japan centers in the Bank of Japan."

31. Marquis Katsura, op. cit., p. 122.

32. Ibid., p. 130; Sprague, op. cit., p. 187.

33. Prior to 1890 only the Bank of Japan, the Yokohama Specie Bank, and the national banks were established by special laws and subject to government regulation. The private banks and quasi banks were not then subject to a banking law. In 1890, general bank regulations were promulgated, to take effect in 1893. "By the new regulations the banking business was clearly defined, and all those engaged in that and similar business were brought under special contract by those regulations.... The necessity of creating a banking center in order to facilitate the management of national finance, and the importance of government control and supervision and of insuring a wholesome development, were what led to the new regulations" (Marquis Katsura, op. cit., p. 134). For an account of the subsequent development of commercial banks in Japan, up until 1914, see Patrick, op. cit., With the subsequent establishment, by the government, of specialist banks—the Hypothec Bank and the Agricultural and Industrial Bank in 1896, modeled after the Crédit Foncier; the Industrial Bank in 1900, modeled after the Crédit Mobilier; and banks for special areas, Taiwan and Hokkaido—the Japanese banking system had a full range of banking institutions at the start of the twentieth century (see "The Banking System of Japan" and Patrick, op. cit., passim).

34. Sprague, op. cit., p. 192.

35. Ibid., p. 192.

36. Sprague, op. cit., p. 210:

> Another expectation from the establishment of the Bank of Japan was the equalization of rates throughout the country. This was not realized during the first twenty years of its history. The bank lent at different rates at its various branches and charged a premium on exchange to prevent the proceeds of loans made where its rate was low from being transferred to localities where its rate was high. In 1906 this practice was changed, apparently not as a result of anything which had been accomplished by the bank itself but, because with the development of banking facilities furnished by other banks, rates had of themselves become more even throughout the country.

Patrick, op. cit., p. 266, however, records regional disparities in interest rates continuing in 1914. Since 1883, the Bank of Japan did, however, begin to enlarge a nationwide network of domestic exchange settlement by promoting correspondent contacts with commercial banks; and it also made efforts to encourage the general use of commercial bills as payment facilities since 1882, when the act concerning bills of exchange and promissory notes was proclaimed.

37. Op. cit., p. 192.
38. Marquis Katsura, op. cit., pp. 123–124; also see Sprague, op. cit., p. 185.
39. Ibid., p. 125.
40. In fact the operations of the Bank began slowly, since it did not obtain the wherewithal to operate from the transfer of reserves from the national banks until 1884/85—see Sprague, op. cit., p. 187.
41. Ibid., pp. 190, 212.
42. Ibid., pp. 209–210.
43. Ibid., pp. 209–210.
44. Prior to 1905 (ibid., p. 202),

> The Bank of Japan, however, probably could not have granted loans more freely with advantage to the business community and consistent with its own safety. Until the recent war with Russia the specie reserve of the Bank was hardly sufficient to permit expansion. During the period between 1900 and 1904 the issue of notes was frequently beyond the untaxed limit of 120,000,000 yen above specie holdings. Moreover, the ratio of reserve to demand obligations (deposits and notes) was during much of the time under 30 per cent, a ratio certainly not large considering the responsibilities of the Bank. Directly after the war the reserve of the Bank was much enlarged from the proceeds of foreign loans negotiated by the Government, but the extension of operations by the Bank at that time was out of the question. Rendered optimistic by successes in war and a rather fictitious abundance of capital, the business community, including most of the other banks, engaged for nearly two years in wild and reckless activities, which culminated in the latter part of 1907 in a general collapse, followed by a period of depression which has hardly reached its term at the present time.

45. Op. cit., p. 253; also see p. 274.
46. Sprague, op. cit., p. 191.
47. Ibid., pp. 204–205.
48. Baron Sakatani, op. cit., p. 145. Also see Naruse, op. cit., p. 163; "We believe that, in this respect [various kinds of banks to satisfy differing needs], our system of monetary organs is perfect."

Bibliography

Acheson, K., and Chant, J. F. (1973). "Bureaucratic Theory and the Choice of Central Bank Goals," *Journal of Money, Credit, and Banking*, Vol. 5.

Aharony, J., and Swary, I. (1983). "Contagion Effects of Bank Failures: Evidence from Capital Markets," *Journal of Business*, Vol. 56, No. 3, 305–322.

Bagehot, W. (1927/1973). *Lombard Street* (London: Kegan, Paul & Co., 1973); references from 14th Ed. (London: John Murray, 1927).

Barclay, C. R. (1978). "Competition and Financial Crisis—Past and Present," *Competition and Regulation of Banks*, ed. J. Revell, Bangor Occasional Papers in Economics No. 14 (University of Wales Press).

Baron, D. (1982). "A Model of the Demand for Investment Banking and Advising and Distribution Services for New Issues," *Journal of Finance*, Vol. 37, No. 4, 955–976.

Barth, J. R., and Keleher, R. E. (1984). "Financial Crisis and the Role of the Lender of Last Resort," *Federal Reserve Bank of Atlanta Economic Review*, Vol. 69, No. 1, 58–67.

Benston, G. J. (1983). "Deposit Insurance and Bank Failures," *Federal Reserve Bank of Atlanta Economic Review*.

Benston, G. J., Eisenbeis, R. A., Horvitz, P. M., Kane, E. J., and Kaufman, G. G. (1986). *Perspectives on Safe and Sound Banking: Past, Present, and Future* (Cambridge, MA: MIT Press,).

Bernanke, B. S. (1983). "Non-Monetary Effects of the Financial Crisis in the Propagation of the Great Depression," *American Economic Review*, Vol. 73, No. 3, 257–276.

Bryant, R. (1983). "Eurocurrency Banking: Alarmist Concerns and Genuine Issues," *Brookings Discussion Papers in International Economics*, No. 2.

Buchanan, J. M. (1984). "Can Policy Activism Succeed? A Public Choice Perspective," Federal Reserve Bank of St. Louis Conference on The Monetary vs. Fiscal Policy Debate, mimeo.

Cagan, P. (1963). "The First Fifty Years of the National Banking System," chapter 2 in *Banking and Monetary Studies*, ed. D. Carson (Homewood, IL: Irwin).

Cameron, R. (1967). *Banking in the Early Stages of Industrialization* (New York: Oxford University Press).

Cameron, R., ed. (1972). *Banking and Economic Development* (New York: Oxford University Press).

Canovai, T., and Ferraris, C. F. (1911). "Italian Banks of Issue," Senate Document No. 575 in *Banking in Italy, Russia, Austro-Hungary and Japan*, National Monetary Commission, Vol. XVIII (Washington, DC: Government Printing Office).

Carson, D., ed. (1963). *Banking and Monetary Studies* (Homewood, IL: Irwin).

Chant, J. F. (1987). "Regulation of Financial Institutions—a Functional Analysis," *Bank of Canada Technical Report*., No. 45.

Chant, J. F., and Acheson, K. (1972). "The Choice of Monetary Instruments and the Theory of Bureaucracy," *Public Choice*, Vol. 12.

Chant, J. F., and Acheson, K. (1973). "Mythology and Central Banking," *Kyklos* Vol. 26, No. 2.

Checkland, S. G. (1975). *Scottish Banking: A History, 1695–1973* (Glasgow: Collins).

Cohen, J. S. (1972) "Italy 1861–1914," chapter III in *Banking and Economic Development*, ed. R. Cameron (New York: Oxford University Press).

Conant, C. A. (1911). "The National Bank of Belgium," Senate Document No. 400 in *Banking in Belgium and Mexico*, National Monetary Commission, Vol. XVI (Washington, DC: Government Printing Office).

Congdon, T. (1981). "Is the Provision of a Sound Currency a Necessary Function of the State?" *National Westminster Quarterly Review*.

Cornwell, R. (1983). *God's Banker, an Account of the Life and Death of Roberto Calvi* (London: Victor Gollancz Ltd.).

Council of Economic Advisers (1984). *The Annual Report of the Council of Economic Advisers* (Washington, DC: US Government Printing Office).

Crawford, P. (1982). Discussion of Guttentag and Herring paper "The Insolvency of Financial Institutions" in *Crises in the Economic and Financial Structure*, ed. P. Wachtel (Lexington, MA: D. C. Health).

Currie, D., Cowen, T., Furstenberg, G., Goodhart, G., Pearce, I., and Tideman, N. (1986). "Symposium on Hayek's 'Standard,'" *Economic Affairs*, Vol. 6, No. 5.

Diamond, D. W. (1984). "Financial Intermediation and Delegated Monitoring," *Review of Economic Studies*, Vol. 51, No. 3, 393–414.

Diamond, D. W. and Dybvig, P. H. (1983). "Bank Runs, Deposit Insurance, and Liquidity," *Journal of Political Economy*, Vol. 91, No. 3, 401–419.

Dorrance, G. S. (1952). "The Bank of Canada," *Banking in the British Commonwealth*, ed. R. S. Sayers (Oxford: Oxford University Press).

Duncan, G. A. (1952). "Banking in Ireland," *Banking in the British Commonwealth*, ed. R. S. Sayers, (Oxford: Oxford University Press).

Fama, E. F., (1980). "Banking in the Theory of Finance," *Journal of Monetary Economics*, No. 6.

Fama, E. F. (1981). "Commodity and Fiduciary Standards," manuscript.

Federal Deposit Insurance Corporation (1983). *Deposit Insurance in a Changing Environment: A Study of the Current System of Deposit Insurance Pursuant to Section 712 of the Garn-St. Germain Depository Institution Act of 1982. Submitted to the United States Congress by the Federal Deposit Insurance Corporation* (Washington, DC: Federal Deposit Insurance Corporation).

Federal Reserve Bank of Chicago (1986). *Proceedings of a Conference on Bank Structure and Competition* (Chicago: FRB).

Fetter, F. W. (1965). *Development of British Monetary Orthodoxy, 1797–1875* (Cambridge, MA: Harvard University Press).

Flannery, M. J. (1982) "Deposit Insurance Creates, a Need for Bank Regulation," *Federal Reserve Bank of Philadelphia Business Review*.

Flannery, M. J., and Guttentag, J. M. (1980). "Problem Banks: Examination, Identification, and Supervision," *State and Federal Regulation of Commercial Banks*, ed. L. Lapidus et al. (Washington, DC: FDIC).

Flux, A. W. (1911). "The Swedish Banking System," Senate Document No. 576 in *Banking in Sweden and Switzerland*, National Monetary Commission, Vol. XVII (Washington, DC: Government Printing Office).

Fraser, D. R., and McCormack, J. P. (1978). "Large Bank Failures and Investor Risk Perceptions: Evidence from the Debt Market," *Journal of Financial and Quantitative Analysis*, Vol. 13, No. 3.

Friedman, M. A. (1959). *A Program for Monetary Stability* (New York: Fordham University).

Friedman, M. A. (1982). "Monetary Policy: Theory and Practice," *Journal of Money, Credit, and Banking*, Vol. 14.

Friedman, M. A. (1984). "Currency Competition: A Sceptical View." parts 1 and 2 of chapter I, "The Theory of Currency Competition," in *Currency Competition and Monetary Union*, ed. P. Salin (The Hague: Martinus Nijhoff).

Friedman, M. A., and Schwartz, A. J. (1963). *A Monetary History of the US 1867–1960* (Princeton: Princeton University Press).

Gardener, E. P. M. "Legal Rules versus 'Vicarious Participation' in Bank Prudential Regulation," *Competition and Regulation of Banks*, ed. J. Revell, Bangor Occasional Papers in Economics No. 14 (University of Wales Press).

Goodhart, C. A. E. (1969). *The New York Money Market and the Finance of Trade, 1900–1913 (Cambridge, MA: Harvard University Press)*.

Goodhart, C. A. E. (1972). *The Business of Banking, 1891–1914* (London: Weidenfeld and Nicolson).

Goodhart, C. A. E. (1985). *The Evolution of Central Banks*, STICERD Monograph, London School of Economics.

Goodhart, C. A. E. (1987a). "Why Do Banks Need a Central Bank?" *Oxford Economic Papers*, Vol. 39.

Goodhart, C. A. E. (1987b). "Financial Regulation and Supervision: A Review of Three Books," *National Westminster Bank Quarterly Review*.

Goodman, L. S. (1982). "On the Interaction between Bank Risk and the Lender of Last Resort," Federal Reserve Bank of New York Research Paper No. 8224.

Goodman, L. S., and Shaffer, S. (1983). "The Economics of Deposit Insurance: A Critical Evaluation of Proposed Reforms," Federal Reserve Bank of New York Research Paper No. 8308.

Greenfield, R. L., and Yeager, L. B. (1983). "A Laissez-Faire Approach to Monetary Stability," *Journal of Money, Credit, and Banking*, Vol. 15, No. 3.

Group of Thirty (1982). *How Bankers See the World Financial Market* (New York: Group of Thirty).

Gunasekera, H. A. de S. (1962). *From Dependent Currency to Central Banking in Ceylon* (London: G. Bell and Sons Ltd.).

Guttentag, J. M., and Herring, R. (1982a). "The Insolvency of Financial Institutions: Assessment and Regulatory Disposition," Chapter 4 in *Crises in Economic and Financial Structure*, ed. P. Wachtel (Lexington, MA: D. C. Heath).

Guttentag, J. M., and Herring, R. (1982b). "A Framework for the Analysis of Financial Disorder," chapter 4 in *Economic Activity and Finance*, eds. M. Blume, J. Crockett, and P. Taubman, (Cambridge, MA: Bellinger).

Guttentag, J. M., and Herring, R. (1983). "The Lender-of-Last-Resort Function in an International Context," *Princeton Studies in International Finance*, No. 151 (Princeton: Princeton University Press).

Guttentag, J. M., and Herring, R. (1984). "Strategic Planning by International Banks to Cope with Uncertainty," mimeo.

Hayek, F. A. (1937). *Monetary Nationalism and International Stability* (London: Longmans Green).

Hayek, F. A. (1960). *The Constitution of Liberty* (Chicago: University of Chicago Press).

Hayek, F. A. (1976a). "Choice in Currency: A Way to Stop Inflation," *The Institute of Economic Affairs*, Occasional Paper 48.

Hayek, F. A. (1976b). *Denationalization of Money* (London: Institute of Economic Affairs).

Hayek, F. A. (1978). *Denationalization of Money—the Argument Refined* (London: Institute of Economic Affairs).

Hayek, F. A. (1984). "The Future Unit of Value," part I. 1 of Chapter I, "The Theory of Currency Competition," in *Currency Competition and Monetary Union*, ed P. Salin (The Hague: Martinus Nijhoff).

Hayek, F. A. (1986). "Market Standards for Money," *Economic Affairs*, Vol. 6, No. 4.

Hirsch, F. (1977). "The Bagehot Problem," *The Manchester School of Economic and Social Studies*, Vol. 45, No. 3.

Horvitz, P. M. (1975). "Failures of Large Banks: Implications for Banking Supervision and Deposit Insurance," *Journal of Financial and Quantitative Analysis*, Vol. 10.

Humphrey, T. M. (1975) "The Classical Concept of the Lender of Last Resort," *Federal Reserve Bank of Richmond Economic Review*, Vol. 61.

Jao, Y. C. (1983). "A Libertarian Approach to Monetary Theory and Policy," Department of Economics, University of Hong Kong, Discussion Paper No. 23.

Johnson, J. F. (1910). *The Canadian Banking System*, National Monetary Commission Monograph, 61st Congress, 2nd Session, Senate Document No. 583.

Kane, E. J. (1984). "Regulatory Structure in Futures Markets: Jurisdictional Competition among the SEC, the CFTC, and Other Agencies," National Bureau of Economic Research Working Paper No. 1331.

Kane, E. J. (1985). *The Gathering Crisis in Federal Deposit Insurance* (Cambridge, MA: MIT Press).

Kareken, J. H. (1981). "Deregulating Commercial Banks: The Watchword Should Be Caution," *Federal Reserve Bank of Minneapolis Quarterly Review*.

Kareken, J. H. (1983). "Deposit Insurance Reform or Deregulation Is the Cart Not the Horse," *Federal Reserve Bank of Minneapolis Quarterly Review*.

Kareken, J. H., and Wallace, N. (1978). "Deposit Insurance and Bank Regulation: A Partial-Equilibrium Exposition," *Journal of Business*, Vol. 51, No. 3.

Katsura, Marquis, et al. (1911). "The Banking System of Japan," in "Banking in Russia, Austro-Hungary, Holland and Japan," Senate Document No. 586 in *Banking in Italy, Russia, Austro-Hungary and Japan*, National Monetary Commission, Vol. XVIII (Washington, DC: Government Printing Office).

Kaufman, G. G. (1987). "The Truth about Bank Runs," FRB Chicago Staff Memoranda SM-87-3.

Keynes, J. M. (1931). *Essays in Persuasion* (London).

Kindleberger, C. P. (1984). *A Financial History of Western Europe* (London: George Allen & Unwin).

King, R. G. (1983). "On the Economics of Private Money," *Journal of Monetary Economics*, Vol. 12, No. 1.

Klein, B. (1974). "The Competitive Supply of Money," *Journal of Money, Credit, and Banking*, Vol. 6, No. 4.

Klein, B. (1976). "A Comment on Tullock's 'Competing Monies,'" *Journal of Money, Credit, and Banking*, Vol. 8, No. 4.

Korobow, L., Stuhr, D. P., and Martin, D. (1977). "A Nationwide Test of Early Warning Research in Banking," *Federal Reserve Bank of New York Quarterly Review*.

Landmann, J. (1911). "The Swiss Banking Law," Senate Document No. 401 in *Banking in Sweden and Switzerland*, National Monetary Commission, Vol. XVII (Washington, DC: Government Printing Office).

Leijonhufvud, A. (1983). "Constitutional Constraints on the Monetary Powers of Government," *Economia delle Scelte Pubbliche* (*Journal of Public Finance and Public Choice*), No. 2.

Leland, H. E., and Pyle, D. H. (1977). "Information Asymmetries, Financial Structure and Financial Intermediaries," *Journal of Finance*, Vol. 32, No. 2, 371–387.

Liesse, A. (1911). "Evolution of Credit and Banks in France," Senate Document No. 522 in *Banking in France and the French Bourse*, National Monetary Commission, Vol. XV (Washington, DC: Government Printing Office).

Lombra, Raymond, and Moran, M. (1980). "Policy Advice and Policy-Making at the Federal Reserve," in *Carnegie-Rochester Conference on Public Policy*, No. 13, eds. K. Brunner and A. Meltzer (*Supplement to Journal of Monetary Economics*).

Marais, D. A. J. (1979). "A Method of Quantifying Companies' Relative Financial Strength," Bank of England Discussion Paper No. 4.

Matthews, R. C. O. (1954). *A Study in Trade-Cycle History: Economic Fluctuations in Great Britain, 1833–1842* (Cambridge: Cambridge University Press).

Mayer, T. (1982). "Federal Reserve Policy in the 1973–1975 Recession: A Case Study of Fed Behavior in a Quandary," chapter 8 in *Crises in the Economic and Financial Structure*, ed. P. Wachtel (Lexington, MA: D. C. Heath).

McCallum, B. T. (1985). "Bank Deregulation, Accounting Systems of Exchange, and the Unit of Account: A Critical Review," *Carnegie-Rochester Conference Series on Public Policy*, Vol. 23.

McCarthy, I. S. (1980). "Deposit Insurance: Theory and Practice," *IMF Staff Papers*, Vol. 27.

McMahon, C. W. (1984). "The Business of Financial Supervision," *Bank of England Quarterly Bulletin*, Vol. 24, No. 1.

Meltzer, A. H. (1983). "Monetary Reform in an Uncertain Environment," *Cato Journal*, Vol. 3, No. 1.

Money Trust Investigation (1912/13). Familiar name for the publication by the United States House of Representatives, *Investigation of the Financial and Monetary Conditions in the United States*, under House Resolutions Nos. 429 and 504 before the Subcommittee on Banking and Currency (also known as the Pujo Investigation), 2 Vols., 29 parts (Washington, DC: Government Printing Office).

Moran, M. (1984), *The Politics of Banking* (London: Macmillan Press).

National Monetary Commission (1911a). *The English Banking System*, Vol. VIII (Washington, DC: Government Printing Office).

National Monetary Commission (1911b), *Banking in Canada*, Vol. IX (Washington, DC: Government Printing Office).

National Monetary Commission (1911c). *The Reichsbank and Renewal of Its Charter*, Vol. X (Washington, DC: Government Printing Office).

National Monetary Commission (1911d) *Articles on German Banking and German Banking Laws*, Vol. XI (Washington, DC: Government Printing Office).

National Monetary Commission (1911e). *The German Bank Inquiry of 1908 (Stenographic Reports)*, Vol. XII, part 1, and Vol. XIII, part 2 (Washington, DC: Government Printing Office).

National Monetary Commission (1911f). *The Great German Banks*, Vol. XIV (Washington, DC: Government Printing Office).

National Monetary Commission (1911g). *Banking in France and the French Bourse*, Vol. XV (Washington, DC: Government Printing Office).

National Monetary Commission (1911h). *Banking in Belgium and Mexico*, Vol. XVI (Washington, DC: Government Printing Office).

National Monetary Commission (1911i). *Banking in Sweden and Switzerland*, Vol. XVII (Washington, DC: Government Printing Office).

National Monetary Commission (1911j). *Banking in Italy, Russia, Austro-Hungary and Japan*, Vol. XVIII (Washington, DC: Government Printing Office).

National Monetary Commission (1911k). *Administrative Features of National Banking Laws and European Fiscal and Postal Savings Systems*, Vol. XIX (Washington, DC: Government Printing Office).

Noyes, A. D. (1909). *Forty Years of American Finance: 1865–1907* (New York: G. P. Putnam's Sons).

Parnell, H., Sir (1827). *Observations on Paper Money, Banking and Overtrading, Including Those Parts of the Evidence Taken before the Committee of the House of Commons Which Explained the Scotch System of Banking*, pamphlet.

Patron, M. (1911). "The Bank of France in Its Relation to National and International Credit," Senate Document No. 494, in *Banking in France and the French Bourse*, National Monetary Commission, Vol. XV (Washington, DC: Government Printing Office).

Pettway, R. H. (1980). "Potential Insolvency, Market Efficiency, and Bank Regulation of Large Commercial Banks," *Journal of Financial and Quantitative Analysis*, Vol. 15, No. 1.

Pettway, R. H., and Sinkey, J. F., Jr. (1980). "Establishing On-Site Bank Examination Priorities: An Early-Warning System Using Accounting and Market Information," *Journal of Finance*, Vol. 35, No. 1.

Prussing, E. E. (1907). National Banks and the Trust Company Problem," *Practical Problems in Banking and Currency*, ed. W. H. Hull (New York: Macmillan).

Reichsbank, The (1911). "The Reichsbank, 1876–1900," Senate Document No. 408, *The Reichsbank and Renewal of its Charter*, National Monetary Commission, Vol. X (Washington, DC: Government Printing Office).

Revell, J. R. S. (1975). *Solvency and Regulation of Banks*, Bangor Occasional Papers in Economics No. 5 (University of Wales Press).

Revell, J. R. S. (1976). "Reforming UK Bank Supervision," *The Banker*, Vol. 126, No. 606.

Revell, J. R. S. (1978). *Competition and Regulation of Banks*, Bangor Occasional Papers in Economics No. 14 (University of Wales Press).

Rockoff, H. (1974). "The Free Banking Era: A Re-Examination," *Journal of Money, Credit, and Banking*, Vol. 6, No. 2.

Rockoff, H. (1975). *The Free Banking Era: A Reconsideration* (New York: Arno Press).

Rolnick, A. J., and Weber, W. (1983). "New Evidence on the Free Banking Era," *American Economic Review*, Vol. 73.

Rudolph, R. L. (1972). "Austria 1800–1914," chapter II in *Banking and Economic Development*, ed. R. Cameron (New York: Oxford University Press).

Salin, P. (1984a), "General Introduction," *Currency Competition and Monetary Union*, ed. P. Salin (The Hague: Martinus Nijhoff).

Salin, P., ed. (1984b). *Currency Competition and Monetary Union* (The Hague: Martinus Nijhoff).

Sandler, T., and Tschirhart, J. T. (1980). "The Economic Theory of Clubs: An Evaluation Survey," *Journal of Economic Literature*, Vol. 18.

Santoni, G. J. (1984). "A Private Central Bank: Some Olde English Lessons," *Federal Reserve Bank of St. Louis Review*, Vol. 66, No. 4.

Schwartz, P. (1984). "Central Bank Monopoly in the History of Economic Thought: A Century of Myopia in England," from chapter III in "The History of Monetary Thought on Currency Competition" in *Currency Competition and Monetary Union*, ed. P. Salin (The Hague: Martinus Nijhoff).

Schughart, W. F., II, and Tollinson, R. D. (1983). "Preliminary Evidence on the Use of Inputs by the Federal Reserve System," *American Economic Review*, Vol. 73, No. 3.

Selgin, G. A., and White, L. H. (1987). "The Evolution of a Free Banking System," *Economic Inquiry*, Vol. 25.

Shenfield, A. (1984). "Comment on Professor Vaubel's Paper on 'Private Competitive Note Issue in Monetary History,'" chapter II.2, "The History of Currency Competition," in *Currency Competition and Monetary Union*, ed. P. Salin (The Hague: Martinus Nijhoff).

Short, E. D., and O'Driscoll, G. P., Jr. (1983). "Deregulation and Deposit Insurance," *Federal Reserve Bank of Dallas Economic Review.*

Silverberg, S. C. (1980). "Implications of Changes in the Effective Level of Deposit Insurance Coverage," in *Proceedings of a Conference on Banks Structure and Competition* (Chicago: Federal Reserve Bank of Chicago).

Simkin, C. G. F. (1952). "Banking in New Zealand," *Banking in the British Commonwealth*, ed. R. S. Sayers (Oxford: Oxford University Press).

Sinkey, J. F., Jr. (1977). "Identifying Large Problem/Failed Banks: The Case of Franklin National Bank of New York," *Journal of Financial and Quantitative Analysis*, Vol. 12, No. 4.

Smith, Vera C. (1936). *The Rationale of Central Banking* (London: P. S. King & Son Ltd).

Solomon, A. M. (1984). "Remarks before the 56th Annual Mid-Winter Meeting of the New York State Bankers Association," Thursday, January 26, 1984, Federal Reserve Board of New York, mimeo.

Sprague, O. M. W. (1910). *History of Crises Under the National Banking System*, National Monetary Commission, 61st Congress, 2nd Session, Senate Doc. No. 538 (Washington, DC: Government Printing Office).

Steering Committee (Report of a System Committee) (1971). *Reappraisal of the Federal Reserve Discount Mechanism, Board of Governors of the Federal Reserve System*, Vol. 1 (Washington, DC: Government Printing Office).

Stiglitz, J. E., and Weiss, A. M. (1981). "Credit Rationing in Markets with Imperfect Information," *American Economic Review*, Vol. 71, No. 3, 393–410.

Stiglitz, J. E., and Weiss A. M. (1983). "Incentive Effects of Terminations: Applications to the Credit and Labor Markets," *American Economic Review*, Vol. 73, No. 5, 912–927.

Summers, L. H. (1983). "Comments on R. G. King's Paper 'On the Economics of Private Money,'" *Journal of Monetary Economics*, Vol. 73, No. 1.

Sylla, R. (1982) "Monetary Innovation and Crises in American Economic History," chapter 2 in *Crises in the Economic and Financial Structure*, ed. P. Wachtel (Lexington, MA: D. C. Heath).

Thornton, H, MP (1802). *An Enquiry into the Nature and Effects of the Paper Credit of Great Britain* (London: Hatchard).

Tiller, R. (1982). "Account Holding in Great Britain," Inter-Bank Research Organization (IBRO), Report No 450, mimeo.

Tilly, R. (1967). "Germany: 1815–1870," chapter 5 in *Banking in the Early Stages of Industrialization* R. Cameron (New York: Oxford University Press).

Timberlake, R. H., Jr. (1978). *The Origins of Central Banking in the United States* (Cambridge, MA: Harvard University Press).

Timberlake, R. H., Jr. (1984). "The Central Banking Role of Clearinghouse Associations," *Journal of Money, Credit, and Banking*, Vol. 16, No. 1.

Tobin, J. (1958). "Liquidity Preference as Behavior Towards Risk," *Review of Economic Studies*, Vol. 25, No. 67, 65–86.

Tobin, J. (1985). "Financial Innovation and Deregulation in Perspective," *Bank of Japan Monetary and Economic Studies*, Vol. 3, No. 2.

Treasury, H. M. (1984). *Building Societies: A New Framework*, Command No. 9316 (London: HMSO).

Trivoli, G. (1979). *The Suffolk Bank: A Study of a Free-Enterprise Clearing System* (London: The Adam Smith Institute.)

Tullock, G. (1975). "Competing Monies," *Journal of Money, Credit, and Banking*, Vol. 7, No. 4.

Tullock, G. (1976). "A Reply to Klein's Comment on Competing Monies," *Journal of Money, Credit, and Banking*, Vol. 8, No. 4.

Vaubel, R. (1984a). "Private Competitive Note Issue in Monetary History," from chapter II, "The History of Currency Competition," in *Currency Competition and Monetary Union*, ed. P. Salin (The Hague: Martinus Nijhoff).

Vaubel, R. (1984b). "The Government's Money Monopoly: Externalities or Natural Monopoly," *Kyklos*, Vol. 37, No. 1.

Viner, J. (1924). *Canada's Balance of International Indebtedness, 1900–13* (Cambridge, MA: Harvard University Press).

Wachtel, P., ed. (1982). *Crises in the Economic and Financial Structure* (Lexington, MA: D. C. Heath).

Wallich, H. (1984). "A Broad View of Deregulation," paper presented at the FRB San Francisco Conference on Pacific Basin Financial Reform, mimeo.

White, L. H. (1983). "Competitive Money, Inside and Out," *Cato Journal*, Vol. 3, No. 1.

White, L. H. (1984a). "Competitive Payments Systems and the Unit of Account," *American Economic Review*, Vol. 74, No. 4.

White, L. H. (1984b). *Free Banking in Britain: Theory, Experience and Debate, 1800–1845* (Cambridge: Cambridge University Press).

White, L. H. (1984c). "Free Banking and Currency Competition: A Bibliographical Note," appendix to chapter III, "The History of Monetary Thought on Currency Competition," and appendix to "Bibliographical Note," in *Currency Competition and Monetary Union*, ed. P. Salin (The Hague: Martinus Nijhoff).

Wilson, J. S. G. (1952a). "The Rise of Central Banking in India," *Banking in the British Commonwealth*, ed. R. S. Sayers (Oxford: Oxford University Press).

Wilson, J. S. G. (1952b). "The Australian Trading Banks," *Banking in the British Commonwealth*, ed. R. S. Sayers (Oxford: Oxford University Press).

Wilson, J. S. G. (1952c). "The Commonwealth Bank of Australia," *Banking in the British Commonwealth*, ed. R. S. Sayers (Oxford: Oxford University Press).

Zuckerkandl, R. (1911). "The Austro-Hungarian Bank," in "Banking in Russia, Austro-Hungary, Holland and Japan," Senate Document No. 586, *Banking in Italy, Russia, Austro-Hungary and Japan*, National Monetary Commission, Vol. XVIII (Washington, DC: Government Printing Office).

Index